A Thesis on the University of Louisiana at Lafayette, the First Higher Education Institute to Desegregate in the Deep South

JUST AS BRUTAL

BUT WITHOUT ALL THE FANFARE

AFRICAN AMERICAN STUDENTS, RACISM, AND DEFIANCE DURING THE DESEGREGATION OF SOUTHWESTERN LOUISIANA INSTITUTE, 1954-1964

RUTH ANITA FOOTE

Book Cover Design and Interior Formatting by 100Covers.

ISBN: 979-8-9909668-3-3 (Paperback)
ISBN: 979-8-9909668-4-0 (Hardback)

AUTHOR'S NOTE

> *"The legacy of 1954 lives on. There is no doubt that these four students and others challenged what was, what had been, and what was to come. And in doing so, they redefined history—a history that was real—and rerouted the destiny of their descendants."*
>
> — Ruth Anita Foote

The preceding quote is an excerpt from my thesis on what African American students experienced—and endured—during the desegregation of the University of Louisiana at Lafayette. In 1954, the campus became the first higher education institution in the Deep South to desegregate as a result of a lawsuit, known as *Constantine v. SLI*. The story of the students is an historical and riveting tale of young men and women—their families, their supporters, and their opponents—in their quest for fair and just education.

I graduated from UL at Lafayette, then the University of Southwestern Louisiana, with a B.A. in English-Journalism in 1982. As an undergraduate, I had never heard about the legacy of Helma Constantine, whose daughter Clara Dell became the namesake for the legal filing. The plaintiffs' suit included four brave young adults and such notable names as future Supreme Court Justice Thurgood Marshall and New Orleans attorney A.P. Tureaud. The legacy also included the university, then the Southwestern Louisiana Institute, which set precedence for desegregation in the southern states. At its helm were President Joel L. Fletcher, Jr., and Registrar James Stewart Bonnet, both named as defendants in the lawsuit.

I did not know about this rich history, nor about Helma Constantine who was our own Rosa Parks, intervening throughout the years to ensure equality for all. I first learned about the *four who would*, and the students thereafter, when I interviewed Helma Constantine for *The Advocate*. She was being honored as the parade marshal for the annual Martin Luther King, Jr. celebration in Lafayette, La. At the time, I freelanced for the state newspaper. And at the time, now in her 90s, she was looking forward to witnessing on television the first African American being sworn in as President of the United States.

Three and a half decades after first graduating, I received my M.A. in History from UL at Lafayette. My concentration was Public History. What follows in the pages ahead is my 2018 thesis as submitted for my master's degree. Only the formatting and the Table of Contents have been changed, and the current copyright and title pages, as well as the Author's Note, have been added. Even though my thesis is available on ProQuest, I decided to self-publish it in a book format as *a keepsake for convenience's sake* so that the story of the students is readily available, and their legacy truly lives on.

Please feel free to connect with me at RuthAnitaFoote@gmail.com or visit me at ruthanitafoote.com.

CONTENTS

"just as brutal ... but without all the fanfare": African American Students, Racism, and Defiance during the Desegregation of Southwestern Louisiana Institute, 1954-1964

A Thesis

Presented to the

University of Louisiana at Lafayette

In Partial Fulfillment of the

Requirements for the Degree

Master of Arts

Ruth Anita Foote

Summer 2018

"just as brutal... but without all the fanfare": African American Students, Racism, and Defiance during the Desegregation of Southwestern Louisiana Institute, 1954-1964

Ruth Anita Foote

APPROVED:

Robert Carriker, Chair
Professor of History

Michael S. Martin
Professor of History

Patricia Lanier
Associate Professor of Management
Chair of the Graduate Council

Mary Farmer-Kaiser
Professor of History
Dean of the Graduate School

To My Mother
Gloria Smyer Foote

ACKNOWLEDGMENTS

I thank my mother, Gloria Smyer Foote, for my love of reading, writing, and history. When I was a child, she told me about the reporters and their radio broadcasts during World War II and inspired my love for history. And I became a Watergate buff because she woke me up each morning so I would not miss the televised Senate hearings. I am grateful to my late father, Joel L. Foote Sr., for relocating the family to Louisiana before he retired from the military. Even though we were wary to come, I have enjoyed my years here and have grown to love the rich culture.

I thank my thesis committee—Dr. Robert Carriker, Chair, Dr. Mary Farmer-Kaiser, and Dr. Michael S. Martin—for their guidance, encouragement, and understanding, especially when life interrupted. I cannot imagine completing this thesis without any of them. I thank them for their faith in me. I thank them also for their patience. When I became a M.A. candidate, Dr. Farmer-Kaiser was the History Graduate

Coordinator; today she is the Dean of the Graduate School. I am grateful that she and the others directed me on this journey.

I thank Dr. Chad Parker and Dr. Kim Todt for their encouragement. I am also grateful for the assistance of the late Dr. Bruce Turner and the staff at Dupré Library's Louisiana Room.

I thank Dr. Michael G. Wade for first documenting "the four who would." And I am grateful for "the four who would" upon whose deeds and memories this thesis exists.

I thank all of my family and friends who have supported me over the years and have encouraged my research. I am grateful to SMILE Community Action Agency for its support and participation in a state training program, which helped to pay for several grad courses.

And not least of all, I thank Peter for his love and support—for being there.

INTRODUCTION

For some African American students, the 1954 desegregation of Southwestern Louisiana Institute began and ended with the beanies—little caps that adorned the shaved heads of freshman students. So synonymous were the beanies with the freshmen, that some might have considered them the freshman mascot. Such were their significance during the era that the beanies became part of the university's legacy, netting a coveted spot in the school's anniversary book depicting its first one hundred years. In its coverage of the third decade, the book—excerpted in the university's alumni magazine *La Louisiane*—notes: "Freshmen were required to wear beanies in the late 1930s. The tradition of wearing beanies continued until the 1960s." To the left of these words, a photograph shows a young white male freshman with a beanie tilted atop his head.[1]

1 Kathleen Thames, "A Look Back at 100 Years," *La Louisiane* (Fall 2000): 17.

What can be labeled as the beanie incident occurred when a group of African American students thought the tradition was also theirs. Their action only illuminated the falsehood and fallacy of the school's desegregation and served as a microcosm of true race relations in the community because it illustrated the consequences of what happened when African Americans veered from a perceived-yet-not-spoken role of insubordination and inferiority. It showed how African American students' desire for inclusion nearly erupted into chaos and reprimand for no other reason than they wanted to belong also. But instead of having their heads shaved by upperclassmen, as was the tradition at the time for their white counterparts, these black young men and other African American students encountered racism and became pawns, even victims, of a discriminatory educational system that one of them pegged as "brutal." And just like the beanies, their story, which covers the first decade of desegregation at the Southwestern Louisiana Institute, was never fully told. This thesis tells that story.[2]

The Louisiana Digital Library documents more photographs of students with the popular SLI beanies. One photograph of a long line, seemingly meandering into infinity, captures beanie-wearing freshmen preparing to go to a football game. Another photograph features a long line of freshmen heading up the stairs with beanies on their heads during

2 Dr. James Caillier, interview by author, March 3, 2013, Lafayette, La., recording, in possession of author; Rachel Emanuel and Alexander P. Tureaud, Jr., *A More Noble Cause: A.P. Tureaud and the Struggle for Civil Rights in Louisiana* (Baton Rouge: Louisiana State University Press, 2011), 183.

registration. Both young men and women wear beanies. And in yet another photograph, three campus girls pose for the camera, the one in the middle flanked by the other two whose accessories include the beanies. But there are no photographs of the beanie incident—the day that a small group of young African American men expected the beanies to become part of their freshman legacy, too, after they registered as students in 1960. Even though six years had passed since the school's landmark desegregation ruling in 1954, that was not to be.[3]

History acknowledges SLI, known today as the University of Louisiana at Lafayette, as the first undergraduate school in the Deep South to desegregate. However, its acclaim as the first came about only because it lost as a defendant in *Clara Dell Constantine et al. v. Southwestern Louisiana Institute et al.*, the lawsuit that led to the school's desegregation and forced admittance of African American students. By default, therefore, SLI found itself as the winner against its southern, white counterparts in an unguided, unwanted, and unwelcomed desegregation race. No school had aimed to outpace their university brethren. Instead, desegregation opponents were convinced that, along with community and state leaders and attorneys, they could usurp desegregation and quash its implementation by complicating matters through racist legislative and constitutional acts, intimidation, threats, and contempt. To thwart desegregation, they had even been willing to pay expenses for African Americans to attend out-of-state schools.

3 University of Louisiana at Lafayette (formerly Southwestern Louisiana Institute) photographs, available online as part of the Louisiana Digital Library, http:/louisdl.louislibraries.org (accessed March 9, 2013).

Whether their actions were due to ingrained fear, pure hatred, or both, they were convinced that race-mixing at SLI's campus could lead to interracial marriage and, in turn, the desecration of white purity in their race.[4]

Southwestern Louisiana Institute's unique status as the first—fostered by *Brown v. Board of Education of Topeka,* but not a product of *Brown*—warrants, and even demands, further examination. It also warrants clarification because SLI's past—and, later, pride—in being the first school in the Deep South to desegregate has become a matter of interpretation. What occurred then, and the indignities experienced by African American students during that first decade, 1954 to 1964, was never recorded from all parties involved, nor was it documented for posterity's sake. Instead history was told by white school officials who took deliberate steps to ensure that their official interpretation of the past prevailed. Even reflections on those days, lacking in redemptive tone, were repackaged and later rebranded, then sealed and cemented by a common denominator, a subtle but solid underlying campaign that maintained desegregation at SLI was not as bad as what happened at other campuses— i.e., Ole Miss's admittance of African American James Meredith, which occurred eight years later in 1962 and left two people dead. Such sentiment echoed through the decades, given voice by both school officials and historians. "Without incident" became the accepted phrase, and somewhat of a rallying cry, whenever mentioning the desegregation of SLI. Through the decades, the one-sided interpretation has served as both justification and denial for how African American students were mostly treated during

4 Caillier interview; Emanuel and Tureaud, Jr., 184-185.

those beginning years. As a result, the black experience of desegregation at SLI was figuratively and literally blacked out.[5]

Only by seeking out new sources, specifically by interviewing African American students left out of the equation, can desegregation at SLI be understood fully. Documenting the experiences of black students—and white students—becomes more and more imperative with each passing year. African American students' desegregation stories must be told and their experiences acknowledged. In doing so, the beanie incident no longer remains one of many tales buried in the recesses of African American minds, aching to be freed. Such interviews also serve as confirmation, and perhaps even as validation, that desegregation did not end discrimination at SLI, nor did the *Constantine* ruling mean black students were being welcomed into the university fold. Instead desegregation heightened racial discrimination and intensified racial exclusion. Black students found themselves receiving lower grades in class than their white counterparts. Social events banned them, and school services denied them access. During the

5 Michael G. Wade, "Four Who Would: The Desegregation of Louisiana's State Colleges/Constantine v. Southwestern Louisiana Institute (1954) and the Desegregation of Louisiana's State Colleges," in *Higher Education and the Civil Rights Movement: White Supremacy, Black Southerners, and College Campuses*, edited by Peter Wallenstein (Gainesville: University Press of Florida, 2008), 60-91; James Stewart Bonnet, interview by Michael J. Foret, no date given, USL Oral History Project, Special Collections, Edith Garland Dupré Library, University of Louisiana at Lafayette, Lafayette, La.; Joseph A. Riehl, interview by Michael J. Foret, June 24, 1981, USL Oral History Project, Special Collections, Edith Garland Dupré Library, University of Louisiana at Lafayette, Lafayette, La.; "Integrating Ole Miss: A Civil Rights Milestone," http://microsites.jfklibrary.org/olemiss/home (accessed May 9, 2013).

university's fiftieth anniversary of desegregation, one African American student even recalled how then-President Joel L. Fletcher spit every time he passed her during those early years. Yet despite these challenges—and others from the white community and even from their own race—African American students coped with racism at SLI and drew strength by supporting one another, developing a grapevine, establishing their own social network, and most of all, keeping focused on their education. But in 1960, a few of these students, specifically the young black men seeking their own legacy while embracing defiance, remained focused on the beanies.[6]

The beanie incident and ensuing consequences, though they occurred six years after the desegregation, were indicative of what African Americans had been fighting for and against during the pre-*Brown* era and the dawn of the civil rights movement when they filed the lawsuit to desegregate SLI. While they saw their actions as a means to inclusion, they also saw desegregation as an opportunity to boost their community spirit. African American educator J. K. Haynes, head of the Louisiana Education Association which had previously funded civil rights cases in the state, viewed the SLI lawsuit as a justified attack on the campus, a preemptive strike that would build "the morale of the community." Haynes encouraged such boldness during his home visits with community activists in Lafayette.

6 Caillier interview; Shelton Cobb and Rebecca Guilbeau Cobb, interview by author, March 3, 2013, Lafayette, La., recording; Shawn Wilson, interview by author, March 12, 2012, Lafayette, La.,

Helma Constantine was among the local activists who embraced Haynes' words and heeded his call to action.[7]

Like Rosa Parks, hailed as the mother of the civil rights movement, Helma Constantine was a local secretary for the National Association for the Advancement of Colored People (NAACP). In 1955, and two states east of Louisiana, Parks refused to give up her bus seat to a white male passenger, an action that led to the Montgomery, Alabama, bus boycott, which boosted Dr. Martin Luther King, Jr. upon the world stage. Yet—a year earlier in the Pelican State—Helma Constantine had already taken a defiant stance by filing a lawsuit against SLI and others on behalf of her daughter, Clara Dell. That lawsuit became one of the dominoes that helped to topple segregation across the Deep South.[8]

Helma Constantine did not mind taking bold stances. She had previously fought against substandard educational resources for African American students at Paul Breaux High School and led a boycott for change that brought national exposure to their cause. But filing the lawsuit against SLI was bolder. By allowing her child to be named as one of the four plaintiffs on the desegregation lawsuit, Constantine let herself and her family become a target like many African Americans across the state and the South who fought for racial equality. At the same time, not all African Americans in the community agreed with her actions. Some feared change and the

7 J. K. Haynes, interview by Doris White, January 20, 1976, Transcript, https://library.louisiana.edu/collections/university-archives-manuscripts/acadiana-manuscripts-collections/miscellaneous-97 (accessed May 23, 2018)

8 Michael G. Wade, 60.

consequences of pursuing it. But that did not deter Helma Constantine. When black cohorts accused her of going too fast, she replied simply, "No—I'm going too slow."[9]

A small group of African American young men, seeking to embrace the beanie tradition, was not slowing down either. While their action could be considered their Rosa Parks moment of defiance, it should more aptly be considered their Helma Constantine moment because the latter's legal actions helped to jumpstart southern desegregation, a year before Parks became a household name, and enabled the young African American men to attend SLI. What matters is that the young African American men refused to surrender their dignity. They refused to surrender their legitimacy. When white upperclassmen told the young black freshmen that they were excused from the freshman tradition—exempted from having their heads shaved and donning beanies—they did what their enslaved ancestors had done centuries earlier with their white plantation masters. They pretended they did not understand. In this case, they pretended that they did not understand what the white upperclassmen meant. Slang terminology today would deem that they had simply "played dumb." Yet in reality, they understood clearly that one of the white upperclassmen had messed up during their registration process, and that was the only reason they had received the beanies. They also understood the implications when another white upperclassman demanded that the young black men give their beanies back. But the African American male students, amongst them

9 Ibid.; Ruth Foote, "History-maker Eager to See History Made," *The Advocate*, January 19, 2009, http://www.louisiana.edu/news-events/news/20040901/50-years-later-desegregation-sli.(accessed May 8, 2013).

Dr. James Caillier, who decades later became Vice President of Academic Affairs at the UL Lafayette and President Emeritus of the University of Louisiana System, refused to give their beanies back. Instead they decided—even though deep down they knew it was not the reason—that perhaps the law prevented the white upperclassmen from cutting black people's hair. They decided it was in their best interest to find a barber of their own race, and off they went in search of Clyde Coco in a black neighborhood, known as The Block in its heyday, which was several blocks from campus. Once they arrived there, Coco shaved their heads.[10]

These young men's action would later shock members of the white community, but it strengthened their resolve and support for one another, invigorating their camaraderie. "After we shaved our heads," Caillier recalled, "we went back to school and we passed downtown. Everyone was looking at us real strange." Their stroll, via a main street, was too much for some white residents and business owners along the way. "Black students with an SLI cap on walking down Jefferson Street—that was unheard of," Caillier said.[11]

According to Caillier, some whites demanded answers during the young men's journey but refused to accept the ones they provided. "'No—you're not students at SLI,'" Caillier recalled them saying. "'It's a white school. Ya'll go to Southern.'" The offended white onlookers may have called the administration for relief from what some perceived as disrespectful—or perhaps, the upperclassmen had alerted the administration

10 Caillier interview; Biographical Profile: James Allen Caillier, President Emeritus of the University of Louisiana System.

11 James Caillier interview.

when the young men refused to give their beanies back earlier. Either way, someone sounded the alarm, because SLI officials were not pleased by the time the African American students returned to campus. According to Caillier, SLI Dean of Men Glynn Abel confronted them: "'Boy—you can't do this. This is not for you. What are you doing with this? You're creating problems for the university.'" Caillier remembers that Abel shook his head, was visibly angry, and then met with other officials to determine "what type of punishment" should be given them. No punishment was meted out, but the reign of the beanie was nearing its end. Two weeks later, Caillier said, there was an announcement that "that practice was discontinued."[12]

There is no known official record about the beanies incident—only the cap's remembrance in the school's anniversary book and the digitized photographs of white students wearing them. Without Dr. Caillier's interviews, history may have never known about the incident that seemingly led to the beanies' early demise on campus. But the occurrence helped to mark the beginning of a new generation of black students not willing to completely accept the racism that their forebears had. For decades, African Americans in Louisiana seemingly accepted racism as part of life—just like African Americans across the South and even nationwide. In doing so, they drank from small "colored only" water fountains, sat in the back of buses, and received meals at the rear doors of restaurants.

Among such forebears was Lafayette's Southern Development Foundation President John Freeman's father, who hid his personal financial successes because he understood jealousy from white coworkers could result in the

12 Ibid.

loss of his railroad job. As a result, Freeman's mother never drove the family's new car to deliver his father's lunch. The forebears also included the late former Southern Consumers Cooperative General Manager Alfred McZeal, who hated telling his children that they were not allowed to eat at the store's lunch counter where he cooked breakfast and swept floors. And then one day, McZeal obeyed his white supervisor and pretended that the lunch counter had always been integrated in order to avoid anticipated sit-ins. Community activist Joe Dennis, who later became a member of the Louisiana Human Relations Council formed to promote racial harmony in the aftermath of SLI's desegregation, was also among the African American forebears who suffered great indignities because of their race, including death. Despite the passing of decades, Dennis remained tormented by an uncle's murder and the fact that no charges and no arrest were made against the known white suspect.[13]

According to historian Adam Fairclough's *Race & Democracy: The Civil Rights Struggle in Louisiana, 1915-1972,* these blacks could be considered descendants of affirmed property, relabeled as "niggers" and "coons" in later generations by Louisiana's white politicians and their supporters who volleyed African Americans back and forth as potential tar babies, hoping racial innuendos and racial slander stuck to their opponents. Denied sanctuary as equal Americans,

13 Caillier interview; Shelton Cobb and Rebecca Guilbeau Cobb interview; John Freeman, interview by author, Lafayette, La., March 13, 2012, recording; Alfred McZeal, interview by author, Lafayette, La., March 3, 2012, recording; Joe Dennis, interview by author, Lafayette, La., March 13, 2012, recording.

equal southerners—denied acknowledgment as full-class citizens—the pre-*Brown* African Americans could do little else but accept their plight. They were more or less, according to Fairclough, at the mercy of the southern power elite.

Likewise, the parents and the grandparents of this new generation of black students had no choice but to accept their second- and third-class citizenship in silence, or suffer consequences. But SLI's first decade of desegregation confirmed that this new generation of African American students were not their parents, and surely not their grandparents. The first decade of desegregation also confirmed that not all whites were woven from the same cloth. Despite prevalent racism and prejudice, some white church and community leaders, university professors, staff members and fellow students risked their reputation, willingly accepted the African American students, and became their brother's keeper.[14]

Fairclough was blunt in his observations, and such candor is warranted when conceptualizing the state aspect of *Brown*, civil rights, and racial rage. However, to understand how such candor fits into the dialogue, we must start at the beginning of this historiography and with what has been considered as the definitive narrative on the landmark case—Richard Kluger's *Simple Justice: The History of Brown v. Board of Education and Black America's Struggle for Equality*. In pondering the impact of *Brown* on "the national psyche" and "the condition of African Americans," Kluger concluded in his 1975 study that

14 Adam Fairclough, *Race & Democracy: The Civil Rights Struggle in Louisiana 1915-1972* (Athens: University of Georgia Press, 1995), 22; Caillier interview; Shelton Cobb and Rebecca Guilbeau Cobb interview; Michael G. Wade, 69, 72-73.

Brown had ended Amore than three centuries of an officially sanctioned mind-set embracing white supremacy and excusing a massive and often pitiless oppression." He noted that the high court had done what no one governmental entity had dared, and as a result, its ruling had "marked the turning point in America's willingness to face the consequences of centuries of racial discrimination, a practice tracing back nearly to the first settlement of the New World." Historian Patricia Sullivan described it like this: "*Brown* hit like a thunderclap." In overturning *Plessy v. Ferguson,* which established "separate but equal," the *Brown* decision "announced a seismic shift away from the nation's long accommodation of the South's racial caste system."[15]

While the Court had taken "a vanguard role" in 1954, its role changed with the release of *Brown II,* which decreased the decision's urgency according to historian Michael J. Klarman. In *From Jim Crow to Civil Rights: The Supreme Court and the Struggle for Racial Equality*, published in 2004, Klarman maintains that the Supreme Court began taking a back seat and did not re-emerge with significance until nearly a decade later. "The civil rights movement had overtaken the school desegregation process," Klarman argues, "and the political branches of the national government were now playing the vanguard role." Klarman, moreover, argued that the impact of *Brown* has been understood in two extremes, from being considered monumental to being considered as having no impact at all. It

---

15 Richard Kluger. *Simple Justice: The History of Brown v. Board of Education and Black America's Struggle for Equality.* New York: Vintage Books, 2004, xii, 780; Patricia Sullivan, *Lift Every Voice: The NAACP and the Making of the Civil Rights Movement* (New York: The New Press, 2009), 420.

is a matter of interpretation of how that decision affected the district federal court's ruling against SLI— which came prior to *Brown.* Its pending existence could not be denied, but the fact remains that the federal court in Louisiana handed down its ruling before the Supreme Court released its landmark decision.[16]

While some historians debated the impact of *Brown,* others began challenging the historical perspectives of the era. In 1980, William H. Chafe localized the desegregation narrative with *Civilities and Civil Rights: Greensboro, North Carolina, and the Black Struggle for Freedom*, which documented the early Greensboro sit-ins that captivated the nation and galvanized the push for racial equality. Chafe believed that "much" of the civil rights literature at the time was negligent in providing answers. While he acknowledged that journalists, public opinion analysts, and scholars had played a significant role in the historiography, they did so at a detriment to posterity. According to Chafe, most studies delineated a national perspective that was removed "from the day-to-day life of the local people most affected by the movement." Chafe noted that "some" historians have even insinuated that actions taken by presidents were instrumental in making a difference. "While all these studies contribute to our understanding," Chafe argued, "very few examined the story of social change from the point of view of people in local communities, where

16 Michael J. Klarman. *From Jim Crow to Civil Rights: The Supreme Court and the Struggle for Racial Equality.* Oxford University Press, 2004, 6-7, 343.

the struggle for civil rights was a continuing reality, year in and year out."[17]

By localizing the narrative, Chafe added African American perspectives, and voices, to the discourse. "Traditionally," he noted, "historians have used newspapers, diaries, manuscript collections, and government documents as a basis for their investigations." As a result, Chafe argued that "until recently, almost all of these sources have represented a white perspective." That had skewed the historical viewpoint and its context. "Simply stated," Chafe further argued, "that perspective cannot do justice to a past that has been multiracial throughout, with blacks as primary actors as well as objects of actions undertaken by others." It is a goal of this thesis to "do justice" in this way to the history of SLI's desegregation.[18]

Fairclough, as mentioned previously, encompassed the Louisiana perspective and its facets in regard to racial equality. But historians have further narrowed the discourse by focusing on the desegregation of higher education and its role in the civil rights movement. Historian E. Culpepper Clark captured the different local viewpoints in the move to desegregate the University of Alabama, known as *The Capstone.* Clark allowed history to judge the actors, whose narratives defined the vital roles they played. He also showed that history was wrought with human emotion and that historical characters acted upon life without justification. While Clark's book defines moments

17 William H. Chafe, *Civilities and Civil Rights: Greensboro, North Carolina, and the Black Struggle for Freedom.* Oxford University Press, 1980, 1, 10.

18 William H. Chafe, 10.

of what happens when plans go awry, his narrative reinforces the importance of localization in the desegregation saga.[19]

What can be noted by these community narratives was that Ole Miss has become the litmus test on the effects of desegregation. When pitting what happened at the University of Mississippi against other desegregation efforts, Ole Miss forever remains tarnished because of the two civilian deaths and numerous injuries that happened after riots erupted once James Meredith, an African American veteran, became a student. While Ole Miss did not impact the African American students who attended SLI during its early desegregation years because it had yet to occur, the tragedies nonetheless play a powerful part in their hindsight. Both students and school officials, interviewed years later in life, made comparisons in regard to Ole Miss and the SLI desegregation. Former African American students considered their experiences just as harsh as what James Meredith endured. On the other hand, school officials were quick to note that their SLI campus had not experienced the same mayhem as Ole Miss. Historians who also analyzed the aftermath tended to echo the school officials.[20]

In *The Price of Defiance: James Meredith and the Integration of Ole Miss*, historian Charles W. Eagles provides a closeup of the racial angst and unabashed superiority in white Mississippians, romanticized by Confederacy charm. Eagles also illustrates a common thread in desegregation and the opposition thereof: the fear of race mingling and a loss of white

19 E. Culpepper Clark. *The Schoolhouse Door: Segregation's Last Stand at the University of Alabama.* Tuscaloosa: University of Alabama Press, 1993.

20 James Caillier interview; Shelton and Rebecca Cobb interview; J. Stewart Bonnet; Joseph Riehl.

purity, which was evident in the desegregation of SLI. Eagles not only critiqued whites for their racist attitudes, but he also pointed out internal problems within the black community and its organizations as well.[21]

Higher Education and the Civil Rights Movement: White Supremacy, Black Southerners, and College Campuses goes further in studying the local lives of desegregation. Edited by historian Peter Wallenstein and published in 2008, the book offers a collection of essays, starting with his "Black Southerners and Nonblack Universities: The Process of Desegregating Southern Higher Education, 1935-1965." The essays range from the desegregation of the University of Georgia to the African American women involved in desegregating higher education. But it is historian Michael G. Wade's "Four Who Would: *Constantine v. Southwestern Louisiana Institute* (1954) and the Desegregation of Louisiana's State Colleges" that laid the groundwork for this thesis. Wade captures the story on the four unknown students whose actions led to the first desegregation of a public higher education institution in the Deep South. Wade's essay and the others added more perspectives into the discourse that ensured historical inclusion. The book reversed what some previous historians had ignored: voices left out of the historical narrative. By incorporating new voices, the essays unsilenced journeys of the past.[22]

This thesis adds yet more voices that still carry the pain of the past, and worry today about its return. Chapter One,

---

21 Charles W. Eagles. *The Price of Defiance: James Meredith and the Integration of Ole Miss*, Chapel Hill: University of North Carolina Press, 2009, 15-18, 31, 443.

22 Peter Wallerstein, 11-14; Michael G. Wade, 60-91.

"What Does the Negro Want?," looks at the question that has been asked through the ages and in a variety of ways. It is a question that should not have to be asked, but it is one that both races have pondered for a long time. Though flawed by its onset, the question and its answer are why African Americans have pursued their quest for racial equality despite the racism they encountered. And in doing so, the question— regardless of its answer—explains why a lawsuit was filed to desegregate SLI.

Chapter Two, "The Desegregation of SLI," examines what happened during the process—the lawsuit, court ruling, early desegregation years and backlash—that led to the admittance African American students and the experiences that they encountered in that first decade. Chapter Three, "Fifty Years & the Aftermath: Reflections and Redemptions," reviews the golden anniversary of the school's desegregation, its reflections and redemptions then and now. The thesis concludes by laying out two schools of historical interpretation in regard to how desegregation occurred at SLI, whether it occurred "with" or "without" incident, and the significance of both.

CHAPTER ONE

WHAT DOES THE NEGRO WANT?

Negro Americans usually feel that whites exaggerate progress; while whites frequently feel that negroes minimize gains.

— Robert Weaver

"What does the Negro want?" has been asked through the ages and in a variety of ways. It is a question that should not have to be asked, but it is one that both races have pondered for a long time. Though flawed from the onset, the question and its answer are why African Americans have pursued their quest for racial equality despite the racism they encountered. And in doing so, the question—regardless of its answer—helps to explain why a lawsuit was filed to desegregate SLI.

Determining the status of African American progress has been a matter of interpretation, a matter of perception. Civil rights leader Robert C. Weaver, who became the nation's first African American presidential cabinet member, was more than cognizant of that fact, particularly when it came to discussing the issue in meaningful and well intentioned conversations between the two races. Appointed by President Lyndon B. Johnson to the newly-developed U.S. Department of Housing and Urban Development, Weaver understood the paradoxical perceptions involved. While there were "many areas of agreement," he noted that there were "also certain significant areas of disagreements." Weaver was one of many black leaders who took pause to assess the status of his race and note for the record its desires and its needs as well as the commitment and the obligation of its leadership. As those before and beside him had done, and those far afterwards likewise would do, Weaver read the pulse of his people and put the particulars in place and in perspective. And then, despite their respective places in history, he amongst others—such as those who had filed suit to desegregate SLI and other schools—confirmed the dismal reality of what was already known, or at least suspected, about the plight of African Americans. In Weaver's case the time was 1963, nearly a decade after the desegregation of SLI and three years prior to his presidential appointment, Weaver delivered a speech, entitled "The Negro as an American," which laid bare the challenges ahead:

Most middle-class white Americans frequently ask, "Why do negroes push so? They have made phenomenal progress in

100 years of freedom, so why don't their leaders do something about the crime rate and illegitimacy?" To them I would reply that when negroes press for full equality now they are behaving as all other Americans would under similar circumstances. Every American has the right to be treated as a human being and striving for human dignity is a national characteristic.[23]

For Weaver, and others who sounded the alarm and committed themselves to helping to overcome inadequacies confronting their race, one thing was certain: the so-called "phenomenal progress" that whites asserted had been gained was not completely reality and instead remained fantasy until socioeconomic gaps were closed and equality became part of the equation. Weaver continued:

Until the second decade of the twentieth century, it was traditional to compare the then current position of negroes with that of a decade or several decades ago. The depression revealed the basic marginal economic status of colored Americans and repudiated this concept of progress. By the early 1930's negroes became concerned about their relative position in the nation.[24]

African Americans had every right to be concerned. After all, they had been comparing themselves only to themselves. Once the assessment process of doing that became obsolete—or rather, inane—it was as if they had eaten from the Tree of Knowledge. They could now see both the good and the bad. And according to the bad, they were way behind their white

23 Robert C. Weaver (Robert Clifton), 1907-1997, "The Negro as an American," program 68, in Digital Collections, Item #5253, http://digital.library.ucsb.edu/items/show/5253 (accessed February 8, 2013.)

24 Ibid.

American counterparts. No doubt learning—and moreover, understanding—their "basic marginal economic status" was a rude awakening. Weaver put it in perspective:

Of course, there are those who observe that the average income, the incidence of home ownership, the rate of acquisition of automobiles, and the like, among negroes in the United States are higher than in some so-called advanced nations. Such comparisons mean little. Incomes are significant only in relation to the cost of living, and the other attainments and acquisitions are significant for comparative purposes only when used to reflect the negro's relative position in the world. The negro here—as he has so frequently and eloquently demonstrated—is an American. And his status, no less than his aspirations, can be measured meaningfully only in terms of American standards. Viewed from this point of view what are the facts?[25]

And then Weaver presented the evidence: African Americans were economically lagging behind their white counterparts as both families and individuals, and that fact served to negate—or at least, deflate—overall historical gains. Weaver said that 1959 figures showed that income for black families was 45 percent less than white families and 50 percent less when it came to individuals. Also, he noted that two-thirds of African American families did not earn enough "to sustain an acceptable American standard of living." Such figures were alarming—and demoralizing. But Weaver was confident that better days were ahead even though he said only six thousand of the one million-plus black families nationwide earned incomes of $25,000 and above at the time. Furthermore, he

25 Robert Weaver.

noted, "Undergirding these overall figures are many paradoxes." One of those paradoxes was that the unemployment rate for blacks at the time was more than double the rate for whites. These figures served as the bleak economic backdrop of what was the state of black America during the early desegregation years of SLI. These figures confirm that African Americans in south Louisiana could not afford the additional expense of sending their children to black colleges out-of-town to further their education when there existed higher education—albeit, white and segregated SLI—within their community radius.[26]

Higher education was also on the mind of Weaver during his speech, and the topic involved "paucity." That was the word he used to describe the number of "qualified negro scientists, engineers, mathematicians, and highly-trained clerical and stenographic workers." What he was concerned about was that most "colored workers"—that is, more than two- thirds of them—were "still concentrated in five major unskilled and semi-skilled occupations, as contrasted to slightly over a third of the white labor force." Also at stake, according to Weaver, was that the "lack of college-trained persons" was more than evident when it came to black men versus black women. Instead of leading the pack, black men made significantly less than their white counterparts whether they were high school or college graduates. But the same plight was not evident when it came to African American women, particularly in comparing black and white women college graduates. For instance, Weaver said that black male college graduates made 38 percent less than their counterparts, while black women made only less than two percent than theirs. He blamed the "lack of

26 Robert Weaver.

economic rewards for higher education" as the reason for "the paucity of college graduates and the high rate of drop-out" among black men. When opportunities were presented for white-collar positions for them, Weaver noted that black men outnumbered black women in completing college. But this paradox was confined to the North, according to Weaver. On the other hand, in the South, where teaching was the predominant field for African Americans, he noted that the reverse was true, and more black women graduated than black men.[27]

The perpetuation of what Weaver described as the "matriarchal" stance, which he noted dated back to slavery in its devaluation of the African American man was still hindering the black population. He considered the perpetuation as the root cause of many of his race's current problems. He said that it had only served to beget negative and harsh consequences, including the denial of the father in the family and the emasculation of the African American man:

There is much in these situations that reflects the continuing matriarchal character of negro society—in a situation which had its roots in the family composition under slavery where the father, if identified, had no established role. Subsequent and continuing economic advantages of negro women who found steady employment as domestics during the post Civil War era and thereafter perpetuated the pattern. This, in conjunction with easy access of white males to negro females, served to emasculate many negro men economically and psychologically. It also explains, in part, the high

27 Robert Weaver.

prevalence of broken homes, illegitimacy, and lack of motivation in the negro community.[28]

Not only had the role of black men been emasculated, but the race as a whole had been attacked and maligned in order to exploit and justify free labor as warranted. Such a belief system legitimized a human being as property in its beginning, and led later to the implementation of the Black Codes, laws restricting African Americans after Reconstruction. The system also encouraged White League groups to sprout like bad weeds, with fourteen in Lafayette Parish at one point—ready to defend Jim Crowism by enforcing segregation and fostering racism. Abolitionist Frederick Douglass, like Weaver would in the century ahead, also discussed the plight of the black man when he rallied white supporters in the North. During one such venture in April of 1865, Douglass delivered a speech entitled "What the Black Man Wants" at the annual meeting of the Massachusetts Anti-Slavery Society in Boston. At the time, according to Douglass, the black man wanted the right to vote and to be viewed as a citizen at all times, and not just during times of trouble. Douglass acknowledged that African Americans were perceived as inferior by dismissing the perception as "old dodge" because it was just a justification tactic. He explained why: "for wherever men oppress their fellows, wherever they enslave them, they will endeavor to find the needed apology for such enslavement and oppression in the character of the people oppressed and enslaved." But whether or not that justification would have rang true—or ever been admitted—when Louisiana served as the role model for southern states eradicating vestiges of black empowerment

28 Ibid.

gained during Reconstruction is unknown. What is clear is that Louisiana was part of the southern culture of states eager to create and maintain Jim Crow. And for three decades, 1930s to the 1960s, Louisiana Senators did just that: they succeeded in strategically stomping out any seedlings that could lead to civil rights. And they quashed legislation that was an affront on segregation. They also fostered a belief that segregation served a peaceful purpose by relegating racial harmony and respect between the races.[29]

These two speeches from Weaver and Douglass, though one hundred years apart, provide an understanding of not only what African Americans wanted as Americans, but also what black men wanted as men. They also portrayed what African Americans were undergoing in a world that most entered by happenstance but were unwelcomed into once they were declassified from being property.

Riddled by paradoxical perceptions, the stage was set, too, for the various viewpoints and desires of the different actors. Whether outrageous or insignificant, heard or ignored, these perceptions played a role in the desegregation of SLI, and determined its discourse despite having no direct intervention.

A good starting point for dealing with these questions on a local level is Harry L. Griffin's *The Attakapas Country:*

---

29 Harry Lewis Griffin, "The White League in Lafayette Parish," *The Attakapas Country: A History of Lafayette Parish, Louisiana* (Gretna: Pelican Publishing Co., 1959), 67; Frederick Douglass, "What the Black Man Wants," April 1865. http://utc.iath.virginia.edu/africam/afspfdat.html(-accessed May 30, 2018); Keith M. Finley, "Southern Opposition to Civil Rights in the United States Senate: A Tactical and Ideological Analysis, 1938-1965." PhD diss., Louisiana State University and Agricultural and Mechanical College, 2003, 14-17, 264-273.

A History of Lafayette Parish, Louisiana, first published in 1959. It is also part of this thesis's historiography. Although a matter of perception, the book provides an early account of African Americans' place within the local scene, their status, and their strength that ultimately led to the desegregation of SLI. It reviews the early history of Lafayette Parish. But Griffin, who served thirty years as the Dean of Liberal Arts at SLI, offers misguided superiority and interpretation. From the book's beginnings, he describes Lafayette Parish's "original inhabitants"—the Native Americans—as living in "miserable" dwellings. He also refers to these Native Americans' descendants as "degenerate," but he acknowledges their bravery.[30] It is evident that Griffin's depiction of races outside the white population requires a deeper understanding and response to its inadequacy.

In Chapter Ten, for instance, Griffin heralds the actions of the White League in Lafayette Parish, almost as if he is documenting their great deeds of the past for posterity. Twelve chapters later in Chapter Twenty-two, Griffin acknowledges the black population.

Even the Native Americans have been given a higher rank by being the parish's original inhabitants in Chapter Two, and as mentioned previously, so has the White League.[31]

Griffin's book documents African Americans and education, from one-room settings to the public school system. It was the first local book that described education for African Americans. This is based upon Griffin noting that the late school superintendent, J. W. Faulk, in his M.A. thesis, "Public

30 Harry Lewis Griffin, 5, 7.

31 Harry Lewis Griffin, 5, 7; https://louisiana.edu/about-us/history/buildings.

Education in Lafayette Parish," had "briefly" mentioned education in regard to Negroes. While Griffin elaborates about black education, he fails to delve into the campus desegregation lawsuit in 1954 even though the book was published only four years later in 1959. The desegregation is mentioned only in passing, noting in parenthesis that SLI has been "accepting qualified Negro students since the fall of 1954." In this case, it is in relation to Griffin explaining the existence of more information from African American teacher Josephine Segura, a graduate student. Griffin notes that she has written "a most valuable term paper" for a sociology class on Negro education in Lafayette. Whether Griffin's information on African American education and its early foundation comes wholly from the Segura's research is unclear.[32]

Griffin explores the life of the black population and notes their achievements in society and accomplishments, as well as the education that they had underwent in mostly one-teacher schools. Griffin describes the businesses, churches, and activities of African Americans in Lafayette Parish. From his viewpoint, they had succeeded. And once again, we are reminded of Weaver's comments on paradoxical perceptions. For Griffin, the "Negroes" appear to have everything they need; their lives lack nothing. We cannot help but wonder what the African Americans would have to say if they could be plucked from history. One of the paradoxes that Weaver noted is obvious in Griffin. While he somewhat boasts about how great life is for the Negro in a chapter that almost seems as an out-of-place afterword, he also seems exuberant in his depiction of the White League. It is almost as if one does not have anything

32 Harry Lewis Griffin, 149-150.

to do with the other. And within his chapter on the White League, he includes an account of the activities of the White League and how they terrorized African Americans, crushing their will to vote.[33]

While historian Adam Fairclough depicts the context of civil rights in the state, and the brutality blacks endured in *Race & Democracy: The Civil Rights Struggle in Louisiana 1915-1972,* we must also look to narratives—books, essays, theses, and dissertations—for the SLI niche and its impact on desegregation. Historians can paint the stage, but without recognizing African Americans as having a legitimate place in society, then their contributions to the discourse are flawed. But without such contributions, even flawed ones, there is no opportunity for measure or for debate. While further research can capture the essence of the era, the accountability of the actors within must not be lacking. However, documenting the past for posterity's sake is not everyone's outright choice. Some would prefer to forget whether from pain, embarrassment, or worry of contamination from the past seeping into their present way of life. Attempts to interview Dr. Fletcher's son were unanswered.

Enough time has passed to present truths and falsehoods. That is why now more stories should be told, and the discourse expanded to incorporate all actors—those known and those unknown. Weaver's commentary that the races viewed racial issues differently is evident in the desegregation of SLI. While some believe that the university fought against desegregation until the end, others believe that the school took action necessary to ensure a smooth transition even though African

33 Harry L. Griffin, 70-71.

American students were placed in a hostile environment. These differences of opinions were not only in regard to campus desegregation, but also have had a vital impact on how racial issues are perceived in America. The two races, whites and blacks, viewed accomplishments and disappointments, or failures, in different manners. That is why Weaver's words could have been written yesterday. After many decades, they remain valid. The pains of the past has not erased them.

The same could be said for the black students at SLI who pressed for desegregation: why were they not satisfied? After all, they had been allowed to attend the school. Yet no one had taken into account, or rather, the accounts failed to acknowledge the indignities that these young students encountered during their SLI tenure. On a local level, "the Negro" and his wants may have been on President Fletcher's mind as well. Perhaps, Fletcher was among those whom authors Stephen J. Caldas and Carl L. Bankston III surmised got a jump on activities when they state in *Forced to Fail: The Paradox of School Desegregation*: "Some institutions, even in the Deep South, could see the handwriting on the wall and began desegregating before the momentous *Brown* decision."[34]

These narratives, therefore, play a vital role in showing what happened for history's sake—to view the situation and make an analysis of the factors at play is important in building one case on top of another. Only in their minds do men remember such days. Joe Dennis can recall the days when African Americans were at the mercy of white people. He remembers

34 Stephen J. Caldas and Carl L. Bankston III. *Forced to Fail: The Paradox of School Desegregation* (Westpart, CT: Praeger Publishers), 27; Michael G. Wade, 66.

how black parents had to keep their children safely in their homes, and themselves as well, on Election Day. Otherwise, they were fodder for disenchanted losers and their supporters who would not spew their wrath on their own race. Instead it was better for them to get drunk and ride into Negro neighborhoods and find black persons to beat up— not because the blacks had even voted, but because the sore losers needed to take their anger and their aggression out on someone, and that someone belonged to a race that they considered inferior whether they had anything to do with the situation.[35]

But African Americans had pride in themselves and wanted to excel, and education was thought to be an escape for that situation. Yet as slaves, they were prevented from gaining knowledge, so too were twentieth century blacks, and they were ridiculed and tormented for trying to do the same. What is lacking today in historiography is the why. That has yet to be examined in depth. It will be up to historians to address. Perhaps what is most blaring is the absence of historical documentation on the desegregation of the Southwestern Louisiana Institute. But in determining what "the Negro" wants is the same as accepting what "the Negro" does not want—a reversal brings forth the right answer.

For the four young adults who allowed their names to be placed in infinity as "the four who would," as historian Michael G. Wade titled his essay on who they were, now was the time to ask the question. What did they want? They wanted an education. As simple as that. Historian Doris White noted in her thesis, "The Louisiana Civil Rights Movement: Pre- Brown Period, 1936-1954," that education was African

35 Joe Dennis interview.

Americans' ticket to freedom. Since early school years, the field had always been a welcome choice in establishing the roots for prosperity and progress. Therefore, these children wanted likewise. And they wanted to see their world better for their offspring. In doing so, unlike others who would renege at the last minute, or be weighed and found wanting, these students saw it through.

Historian Wade describes who they were, beginning with Martha Jane Conway.

According to Wade, she could not afford the expenses to attend school elsewhere. Her dream was to major in business education. Also interested in business was the lawsuit's namesake, Clara Dell Conway. Her goal was "to teach students how to handle their financial affairs more effectively." Wade said that Charles Vincent Singleton, the only adult and male of the four, wanted to enter elementary education. He thought by attending SLI, he could become more competitive, have an edge. According to Wade, Shirley Taylor looked at making a difference in the lives of young people with a law enforcement career. She wanted to focus on juvenile delinquents. Wade wrote that she wanted to attend Atlanta University after SLI graduation. The young plaintiffs were optimistic. They felt the lawsuit would have a positive impact and that was their goal.[36]

Once again, what did the Negro want? He wanted all the same things that white Americans wanted. He was no different, according to Weaver.

---

36 Michael G. Wade, 64.

CHAPTER TWO

THE DESEGREGATION OF SLI

I don't recall anything that was really blatant. But it was there. And you knew it was there.

— SLI Student Rebecca Guilbeau Cobb

The desegregation of SLI was subtle yet sound. Like *Brown,* it came in waves that receded more than they extended. It did not occur just that fall semester in 1954. While it was an eventual process, it began with more than a request for admission. To understand the desegregation of the school, therefore, we must look at what happened during the process— the lawsuit, the court ruling, the early desegregation years, and the backlash—that led to the admittance of African American students and the experiences that they encountered in that first decade. And we must consider what happened prior.

But first, let us examine the subtleties and soundness of racism that some may have considered blatant, and others not—yet they were ones that African Americans understood all too well. For one African American student, they were there every time she passed President Joel L. Fletcher, and every time she greeted him. And every time that he replied by spitting. Not at her. He just spit away from her, and walked on. That was his only acknowledgment that he had heard her, much less even seen her. He was very tall, very proud—pristine. He was also very mean. That was how she remembered him. She also recalled thinking that if she kept greeting him, he might eventually run out of spit. With a sense of defiance, she continued.[37]

"Good morning, Dr. Fletcher," she said. He spit, and walked on.[38]

It was the 1950s, and he was president of the Southwestern Louisiana Institute. And she was among the estimated eighty African American students whom he probably considered as having invaded his white campus as a result of the court-ordered desegregation, stemming from the lawsuit *Constantine v. Southwestern Louisiana Institute*. While he abided by the ruling and had no choice but to allow their admittance, which he may have thought was temporary, he did not mind showing that he "despised that they were there." His spitting was how she remembered him—ingrained in memories that she shared half a century later when she returned by invitation to what had become the University of Louisiana at Lafayette. In her day, it had been SLI, but it was originally the Southwestern

37 Shawn Wilson interview.

38 Ibid.

Louisiana Industrial Institute when the state legislature created it for the education of white children. While her memories of encountering Dr. Fletcher were rekindled during the fifty-year anniversary celebration marking the university's desegregation as the first school in the Deep South to do so, most experiences and documentation remain forever lost because of those who regarded with disdain the events of the day and the early years that followed.

While they failed to circumvent the court's injunction despite pursuit of shameless state legislation and intimidation in the ensuing years, they succeeded in ensuring history would have few primary sources for review. A photograph may have been worth a thousand words for history, but there were no photographs, no words.[39]

Missing from the campus and the community annals have been early official documentation and news coverage on the "first undergraduate desegregation of a previously all-white, state-supported college or university in the South." While being the first to desegregate was a designation that SLI earned for posterity's sake, back in the early 1950s, it was a title that school officials scorned, and a mantle they refused to wear in the beginning. But times changed. On its website today, the university notes as part of its history, as part of its legacy: "in 1954, SLI became the first college in Louisiana to integrate its student body.

The first African American students were admitted without incident, and today UL Lafayette has honored its first African American graduate, Christiana Smith, by naming an alumni chapter after her." Back in 1954, nonetheless, white

39 Ibid.

leaders may have considered even that designation as infamy even though other area schools closely followed in desegregating their campuses. They tried their best to keep it under wrap as their political buddies fought statewide to defy and denounce desegregation, and prevent its dreadful presence on Louisiana campuses. And since these white leaders controlled the power, including the media, it became incumbent upon them to designate history as they saw fit. George Orwell's *Big Brother* would have been jealous—or most likely, proud. But as a result, for a point in time, the rest of the story was silenced, shunned, and figuratively and literally spit on.[40]

In 2012, Clara Dell Constantine Broussard—one of the four young adults whose names were forever a part of the namesake desegregation lawsuit against SLI —died. She had been the last one living of the plaintiffs who tried to become students at SLI during an era that was not too kind to their race. But in 1954, at least publicly, the four young adults and their appeal to become students did not appear to be on the mind of Fletcher when he greeted the new year. In his letter to the alumni in the *Southwestern Alumni News,* he wrote,

"The next few months will be important ones for education in Louisiana." The year of promise was also symbolized by the alumni's "first family" on the January 1954 issue's cover. Alumni President Bernard Marcantel, his wife, and their three toddlers beamed, their faces aglow, perhaps in anticipation of what the future would bring. Like Fletcher, Marcantel also was not publicly preoccupied by pending legal action from

40 Rachel Emanuel and Alexander P. Tureaud, Jr.; "Southwestern Louisiana Institute (SLI)," University History: General. http://www.louisiana.edu/AboutUs/History/General.shtml(accessed May 20, 2018).

African Americans. But he was concerned about the future of white students and whether the state would meet the needs of expanding enrollments. He identified the needs as more facilities and future positions in what he termed as "the complex society, especially in industry, which is being developed in Louisiana." In the year's first issue, Marcantel told his fellow Southwesterners: "1954 will be a crucial year for higher education in Louisiana." There was no doubt that he was worried about what action their political leaders would take. "If our representatives adopt a short- sighted view," he wrote, "Louisiana education will be left in a state of chaos from which it may never recover." He urged the alumni to call their legislators and make sure budget cuts were not in education but elsewhere. His call to action was imperative: "Do it now!" There were no mentions of a possible desegregation lawsuit compounding these matters.[41]

But little did the two men, particularly President Fletcher, realize the far-reaching significance and irony of their words. After all, 1954 became the year of *Constantine v. SLI,* which would forever change their campus colors after its early filing in January. It was also the year of *Brown v. Board of Education of Topeka,* which would impact schools and campuses everywhere. *Brown* ensured that 1954 was the year of change—not only for a campus in Louisiana but for an entire nation. But in that year's first alumni newsletter and the issues that followed, such a future seemed far from the mind of Fletcher. He chose to publicly disregard the present and the fact that there was a lawsuit calling for the SLI desegregation. Instead

41 Southwestern Alumni News, January 1954, vol. 15, no. 4: 3.

of desegregation dismay, his letters to the alumni focused on pushing forward with growth.[42]

So successful was he that even his own son's close friend did not realize local legal action had been taken against the school. Former 16th Judicial District Judge C. Thomas Bienvenu Jr. witnessed the early days of desegregation as an SLI student, and as a friend of the younger Fletcher. On occasion, he even spent time at their campus home. But so low-key were the particulars of the desegregation case that not until half a century later did Bienvenu realize the truth. Bienvenu had always assumed desegregation at SLI was simply the result of the *Brown* case and actions by his friend's popular father. "My recollection of his father was that he was very well liked by everyone in the SLI community, and I kind of thought that he was the one who had done the integration," Bienvenu said.[43]

The history of the four plaintiffs and those impacted remain embodied in the pages of the *Constantine* lawsuit even though it took a half-century for their stories, their histories, their tales to be told—a half-century for them to be printed in the local newspapers. Like Clara Dell Constantine, two of the other three plaintiffs were considered minors—Martha Jane Conway and Shirley Taylor. Therefore, guardian Philip Bourges and mother Effie Taylor, respectively, filed on their behalf. Twenty-one-year-old Charles Vincent Singleton, named as an adult, filed on his own behalf. As the plaintiffs,

---

42 Southwestern Alumni News Southwestern Alumni News, January-March 1954

43 C. Thomas Bienvenu, interview by author, St. Martinville, La., April 12, 2012, recording January 4, 1954.

their case revolved around a simple question: Why should they be forced to travel to Baton Rouge or Grambling to attend segregated schools when there was a campus right there at home? Decades later in her nineties, Helma Constantine would remember how far African Americans had come from segregation. During a 2009 Martin Luther King Celebration, in which she was the parade marshal and guest speaker in Lafayette, Louisiana, told the audience, "You've got a choice. You go where you want to go."[44]

Going where one wanted to go was not the case when the four plaintiffs "presented themselves for admission" before SLI's Registrar James Stewart Bonnet on September 15, 1953—ready and able to pay the school's required fees, and ready and able to prove that they had the credentials to attend. But the Registrar's response signified the one major obstacle they could not change, nor overcome for admissions to SLI: They were "members of the Negro race." And because of that membership, they were denied admission. However, that did not discourage them because it was merely a process in a mission that was much bigger than them, a mission that encompassed their entire race. Ten days later, therefore, on September 25, 1953, they appealed the SLI decision—the denial based on race and color—to the Louisiana State Board of Education. About three weeks later, on October 13, 1953, the Board notified each plaintiff that their appeal was under consideration. But that was all that they did, and seemingly, that was all that they planned to do. The Board failed to follow

44 *Constantine v. SLI*; Tina Marie Macias, "Legacy Lives On; Celebration of King Includes Reflection on Obama," *The Daily Advertiser*, January 20, 2009, Section A.

up on its notification. Its inaction sentenced the appeal to purgatory without prayer. Nearly three months passed, and there was still no word from the Board. It was perpetual inaction—an appeal in limbo—until Attorney A.P. Tureaud filed the local landmark lawsuit on January 4, 1954, effectively ending the silent stalemate and ensuring the Louisiana State Board of Education a complimentary seat in court as one of the defendants in the case.[45]

According to historian Michael G. Wade, "The plaintiffs asserted that, by virtue of its whites-only admissions policy, Southwestern Louisiana Institute was in violation of the 14th Amendment and of federal law, specifically the Ku Klux Klan Act of 1870 (Chapter 114, Sec.16), which provided for the equal rights of all citizens. They based their argument on the Ku Klux Klan Act of 1871 (Chapter 22, Sec. 1), which authorized legal action by any citizen to redress state-sponsored deprivation of rights secured by the Constitution and laws of the United States."[46]

The defendants in the suit included "Joel Lafayette Fletcher, as President, and James Stewart Bonnet, as Registrar of the Southwestern Louisiana Institute," as well the Institute itself. Also named were the officers and members of the Louisiana State Board of Education, as well as the Board itself. Tureaud, described as "Mr. Civil Rights of Louisiana," led the *Constantine v. SLI* desegregation fight—and many, many other similar campus battles— anchored by the NAACP legal defense fund, which included Robert L. Carter and future U.S.

---

45 Clara Dell Constantine, et al v. The Southwestern Louisiana Institute, et al. 4401 Civil Action.

46 Michael G. Wade, 63-64.

Supreme Court Justice Thurgood Marshall, both of New York, and U. Simpson Tate of Dallas. These men signed off on the lawsuit. Among the key players on the *Constantine v. SLI* stage was also *Brown* even though the case's outcome did not make its transforming appearance until the last act, after "the court had granted the plaintiffs' petition for relief" nearly a month prior on April 23, 1953. Following *Brown's* announcement on May 17, 1954, nonetheless, everything changed. Two months later on July 19, 1954, the U.S. Western District Court in Louisiana issued a permanent injunction to the *Constantine v. SLI* defendants, noting that they were "hereby restrained and permanently enjoined from refusing, on account of race or color to admit plaintiffs, and any other Negro citizen of the state, residing in Southwest Louisiana, and similarly qualified and situated, to The Southwestern Louisiana Institute, Lafayette, Louisiana, for the purpose of receiving their training and education in said Southwestern Louisiana Institute." The U.S. Circuit judges were Wayne G. Borah, Ben C. Dawkins Jr., and Edwin F. Hunter Jr. For their actions, historian Rachel Emanuel said that they were considered "nigger lovers."[47]

When the federal court ruled on the plaintiffs' behalf and granted them relief, a large headline in the local newspaper literally rivaled—by twice the size—the amount of content

47 *Constantine v. SLI*; The La. State Board of Education included Eleanor H. Meade, President; Gramercy; Raymond Heard, Vice-President, Ruston; George T. Madison, Bastrop; Joseph J. Davies, Jr., Arabi; Leon Gary, Houma; Alfred E. Roberts, Lake Charels; A.A. Fredericks, Natchitoches; Shelby M. Jackson, Baton Rouge; Isom Guillory, Opelousas; M.M. Welsh, Baton Rouge; Robert H. Curry, Shreveport; Nash Roberts, New Orleans. In time, the defendants were amended to update Heard as president when Meade's tenure ended; Michael Wade; Doris White; Rachel Emanuel, 185.

given to the story. The April 23, 1954 issue of the *Daily Advertiser's* headline blared: "Federal Judges Order SLI To Admit Negro Students." A sub-headline stated: "Court Rules Equal Accommodations Not Available to Race in Area." The dateline was Shreveport. It would take another two months for the court to issue the injunction.[48]

In the years and decades that followed, defining desegregation at the Lafayette campus became a matter of perspectives—the paradigms shifted in regards to race, position, and sometimes, personality. No one was immune, but most fell along racial lines. White university officials emphasized how SLI fared better during desegregation in comparison to other southern universities. In doing so, for instance, they depicted the University of Mississippi as a backdrop for comparison and confirmation that the SLI period of desegregation was tranquil, a description that disregarded—and failed to even consider—the black students' perception or experience. Joseph A. Riehl, vice-president of academic affairs at SLI during the desegregation years, was among them. "I think the integration of Southwestern was one of the most peaceful episodes that took place in that whole unhappy period of marches and Ku Klux Klan and burning of crosses and things of that sort," he said in an interview. Such a comment offers an illusion of historical calm. It does not take into consideration that the *Constantine* lawsuit forced the school to desegregate and the

48 "Federal Judges Order SLI To Admit Negro Students: Court Rules Equal Accommodations Not Available to Race in Area," *The Daily Advertiser*, April 23, 1954.

perils that black students underwent. It also does not take into account that the school did not go willingly.[49]

Riehl and the campus website do not mention that black students at SLI, renamed the University of Southwestern Louisiana in 1960, endured racism on a daily basis, like James Meredith, even though it was a subdued racism. "I don't recall anything that was really blatant," said retired black educator Rebecca Guilbeau Cobb who became a student in 1959. "But it was there. And you knew it was there. You knew how far you could go, and you knew just where you stood." That unspoken non-status of black students, in those beginning years, was a prime reason for differences in opinion between the races. What was also at issue was that desegregation did not bring redemption. According to Cobb's husband Shelton, who decades later served as president of the Lafayette Parish School Board, desegregation did not bring redemption. "Even though everything had gone smoothly in the beginning, there were still vestiges of hostility," he recalled.[50]

Nonetheless, the official word went forth, as noted on the university website today: "in 1954, SLI became the first college in Louisiana to integrate its student body." Even though Riehl mistakenly cited 1955 instead of 1954 as the year of desegregation in his interview, he also acknowledged that the Lafayette campus was "the first public college under the State Board of Education to be desegregated." Yet there were no comments, nor reflections on the fact that a lawsuit

49 Joseph A. Riehl, interview by Michael J. Foret, June 24, 1981, USL Oral History Project, Special Collections, Edith Garland Dupré Library. University of Louisiana at Lafayette, Lafayette, La.

50 Shelton Cobb and Rebecca Guilbeau Cobb interview.

was brought against the campus. It was almost as if the school had willingly desegregated, or moreover, it had volunteered. This assumption was reinforced by university officials. Abel also echoed such sentiment: "And we were the first university in the South to integrate." Abel was even confident to take it another step further, noting that SLI had "integrated with 150 students the first day"—unlike Ole Miss, which desegregated with only one student, James Meredith. Historian Wade, who can be credited with bringing the university desegregation story to light by documenting the four students who filed the lawsuit, puts the early enrollment figure at eighty black students. Like the beanies, however, there exists no available photographs of the event. Yet pictures were taken, according to Registrar Bonnet, who halted that process by asking the newspaper photographer to leave. "He made no fuss about it. He had gotten one or two pictures but I don't believe he ever printed them that I remember," Bonnet said. Mostly likely, he did not. As a result, photo documentation has not surfaced as part of the school's desegregation legacy. That may be why white onlookers were shocked to see the young African American men walking down Jefferson Street with SLI beanies atop their heads.[51]

During her years at SLI and USL, beginning in 1959, Rebecca Guilbeau Cobb estimated that there were fifty to one hundred other black students. In addition to being from Lafayette, the students also came from the surrounding parishes of St. Landry, St. Martin, and Iberia. Those from Lafayette Parish numbered about fifteen students. "There weren't that

---

51 "Southwestern Louisiana Institute (SLI)," University History: General. UL Lafayette website, 1981.

many of us," she recalled. Originally, it had been difficult to gauge how many students were there the first year of desegregation, 1954-1955. President Fletcher had feigned ignorance on the subject. Like the beanie incident, Fletcher was able to maintain that he did not quite know—in this case, the number of African Americans at his school. He may have surmised that actually reporting—or verifying publicly—the number of black students at SLI might scare white students away or increase racial tensions in the community. If anyone asked for the total of African American students that first semester, it would be impossible to relay because according to school officials, Fletcher had forbidden that documentation. Despite the Registrar's insistence, Fletcher had instructed Bonnet not to denote race on the registration cards. "'I positively refuse to let you put race on the registration card,'" Bonnet recalled Fletcher saying. But just like creative accounting, Bonnet was able to bypass Fletcher's instructions, and at the same time, obey his superior knowing one day that he would request the numbers, which he did. Bonnet said that he memorized the black high schools in the area, including the surrounding parishes, and placed small red checks on the side of the cards—a system that only he and his staff understood. "I had about 100 percent effective coverage in that way for the first year," he said. But Fletcher had friends in high places, and a campus reputation and funding to protect as SLI began its countdown to "university" status. Putting race on the registration card would only bring more attention to the fact that the school was racially mixed. In ordering Bonnet not to do so, Fletcher was simply ordering him not to do so publicly. It was a cornerstone of his modus operandi, one that other Louisiana officials would follow when the time came to desegregate their respective campuses. Historian Wade noted that other schools implemented Fletcher's "minimalist approach to handling the desegregation process."[52]

But today in the Fletcher Presidential Papers, in the file on the *Constantine v. SLI* lawsuit, a three-page document has surfaced, entitled "List of Negro Students Fall 1954-55," the first year of African American enrollment, which had been previously estimated at eighty students. The list, noted by its numbered pages, is denoted as being from the Office of the Registrar. Not only does it state names of the seventy-four Negro students, but it also includes their guardian, address, and telephone as applicable. Of the seventy-four students listed, six students are designated as having resigned: the word "Resigned" has been placed in parenthesis after their names. There is no indication of when the resignations occurred. But what is apparent is that most students are designated as being from Lafayette. There are also a sprinkling of students from Abbeville, Breaux Bridge, Crowley, Duson, Jeanerette, New Iberia, Opelousas, St. Martinville, Weeks Island, and Youngsville.[53]

Among the sixty-eight students, who enrolled and did not resign that first year of desegregation, are two of the four *Constantine* plaintiffs, Martha Jane Conway and Shirley Taylor. Other students, listed in alphabetical order, are Shirley

---

52 Bonnet interview; Michael G. Wade, 74; Kristal L. Enter. "Racial Integration in Southern Public Higher Education, 1945-1972, Dissertation, Clare College, Cambridge University, June 2012: 65.

53 Joel L. Fletcher, Presidential Records, 1941-1950, USL Southwestern Archives and Manuscripts Collection, University of Louisiana at Lafayette.

Mae Aldridge, Teletha Mae Aldridge, Lou Mary Alexander, Leroy Joseph Anderson, Ray William Andrews, Claudette Marie Arceneaux, Elnora Theresa Arceneaux, Genevieve Arceneaux, Clarence Thomas Benoit, Louella M. Parker Bernard, Adam Winthrop Bosset, Aaron Junius Boudreaux, Rosa Mae Boudreaux, Priscilla Ruth Bradley, George Breaux, Peggy Joyce Brown, Wendell Ray Byers, Dorothy Mae Caesar, Gloria Louise Clark, Rita Glorine Cormier, Thelma Daigle, Betty Marie Davis, Emma Ruth Dixon, James Drake, Oran Anthony Foote, Alodia Francis, Mary Ruth Gallien, Vera Mae Garret, Junior Weveley Gobar, Lillie Vee Griffin, Johnny Joseph Guigneaux, Arthur Lee Hardy, Shirley Mae Harson, Ollie Mae Harris, Ruth E. Bessard Hayes, Verna Helsire, Juanita Jackson, Timothy Charles Jackson, Mary Belle Joe, Joyce Juanita Johnson, Adelene Jones Jones, Gloria Marie Jones, Lillian Cecelia Labbe, Helen Mae Landry, John Berry Livingston, Irma Jean Minix, Lennart Joseph Mitchell, Charley Mouton Jr., Georgia Haye Mouton, Joseph Mouton, Betty Jane Nathan, Wilma Thibodeaux Peterson, Donald Leo Porche, Mary Theresa Price, Raymond Curtis Randal, Victor Hubert Raphael, Helen Elizabeth Reaux, Audrey Ruth Roy, Mary Loretta Senegal, Catherine Mae Singleton, Geraldine Mae Singleton, Aura Belle Steward, John Harold Taylor, Mrs. Clifton Smith Trotter, Annie Belle Wiltz, and Billy Zachary.[54]

According to African American educator Carlton James, Registrar Bonnet was confident the students would not last at the university. "He took their registration slips and everything and put them in a shoebox on top of the file cabinet because he knew they weren't going to be there long," James said.

54 Fletcher Presidential Records.

"And that was the attitude he had at that time." Moreover, the Registrar's Office was ready. Whether loose lips, friends in high places, neither or both, university officials knew the desegregation challenge was coming before it presented itself. In an interview, Bonnet noted that the school was prepared for the moment. Not only did his immediate staff know what to expect, they knew how to respond. He did as well. When the black students arrived, accompanied by an NAACP field secretary, according to Bonnet, everyone knew what was at stake. Bonnet's staff alerted him, and he alerted Fletcher. "It's happened," he said. And with those brief words, Bonnet confirmed what they had anticipated, what they had been tipped off as to what was going to happen: African Americans had attempted to register at SLI. History-making moments were under way. What further role Bonnet played then and later remains unclear except for his previously noted comments on devising a method for simultaneously obeying and disobeying Fletcher's orders for identifying race, and thereby, realizing the number of African American students. But no matter how many black students registered and attended classes, including that first list of students that founds it way into the annals of history, it was evident that they did not feel welcome. Tolerance, and lack thereof, played a part here. Even a year after the desegregation of SLI , then Governor Robert F. Kennon told the Associated Negro Press, "Our state laws maintain segregation of races." Moreover, *The Plain Dealer* reported that Kennon "seemed surprised and asserted he wasn't aware of the NAACP's demands for desegregation in Louisiana." His comments portray that he was aware of the stance he was taking by maintaining the law of his state.

That was evident. What should have also been evident at the time, Tureaud and the NAACP team were busy filing suits to combat the racist legislative acts being enacted to delay, deter, and demolish desegregation in the state. Desegregation itself had become an actor in politics, determining the course and showcasing the lengths that leaders across the state would take to ensure that segregation thrived despite gains by those favoring desegregation.[55]

The minimalist approach, which Fletcher utilized publicly, played a crucial role in the desegregation of the campus. It served the administration well in their quest to minimize the effects of desegregation. Disregard of the situation, or bleak toleration, ensured that there was little to combat, little to react to, and little to become emotional about. Historian Peter Wallenstein describes these accommodating factors practiced by campus presidents facing change as a "dual tradition of dissent." Wallenstein notes that school officials were forced to balance the past and the present. "In pursuing this minimalist approach to change," he stated, "they sought to navigate between antithetical forces of dissent, and in doing so they managed to blunt calls that schools be shut down rather than desegregated." However, confrontation, even low-key opposition, was inevitable. The beanie incident would not be the last time that the university opted to eliminate an activity to avoid deeper desegregation and to thwart inner integration

55 Carlton James. Oral History Collection. The University of Louisiana at Lafayette Libraries, University Archives and Acadiana Manuscripts Collection, University of Louisiana at Lafayette, Col. 161, Box 4, Tape 1; Lowell M. Trice. "Dixie Governors Say Desegregation Must be Solved on Local Level," *The Plain Dealer*, August 19, 1955, Vol. 57, Issue 33.

that may have even led to violence. In addition, school dances were banned for a time, and intramural sports were cancelled. In both cases, as with the beanies, African American students tried to participate in a school function, only to find themselves met by extreme resistance based upon fear or hatred, or both. Bonnet recognized that fear when white parents pulled their children out of school following desegregation. "Everyone's afraid that you're going to intermarry," he said.[56]

Fear was a tradition in itself, handed down from generation to generation. But Mrs. J. Wallace Lovell of Abbeville decided to acknowledge that fear, or rather her displeasure of hearing that an African American was registered to attend the school. Just before the fall semester, in a letter dated August 7, 1954, to Dr. Fletcher, she voiced her concerns. She wrote that she hoped that he would not allow "the negroes" to attend. She did not want them there with her daughter, who was scheduled to return for the fall semester after being in summer school, because there were "too many things that could happen." Mrs. Lovell also noted that if she were a teacher she would not want to teach them because "you don't know when they might stab you." However, such a racist mindset as portrayed in the letter, did not make the racism any less daunting for the first black students at SLI. "When we first got there, we were shocked to learn we were not allowed to participate in student services and functions," Dr. James Caillier said. These extenuating circumstances may have fueled Abel's extreme reaction to the beanie incident—upset and wanting to punish the African American young men because they dared to follow a tradition

56 Peter Wallenstein, 2-4; Michael G. Wade, 73; Caillier interview; Bonnet interview.

they should have known was not inclusive of them, and as a result, jeopardized the university's heretofore positive image.

School officials could not afford to let anything interfere with that image, nor the intense growth the campus had experienced in its countdown to elevated "university" status.

Therefore, it appears that school officials quashed any threat—even a thirty-year tradition like the beanies.[57]

While the beanie fiasco and other incidents did not result in black students being among those nationwide who "risked life and limb" in pursuit of their education through desegregation, the SLI students still suffered inwardly. While they were not killed in their quest for social justice, they were victims in their own right. "At that time, blacks were treated so badly and you were called names. It was a little rough," recalled Rebecca Guilbeau Cobb. "At SLI, you heard the n-word many times from the other students on campus." While there were no bodies and no bruises, they suffered what could be called psychological abuse. They were students, after all—young adults. They were supposed to be celebrating their best years. At times, they were called derogatory names. On the other hand, they were treated as if they were invisible, as if they did not even exist, denied acknowledgment as human beings—like the main character in Ralph Ellison's novel *Invisible Man*. "No one said anything to us," said Rebecca Guilbeau Cobb. "We just took a seat and we did whatever we had to do and we walked out of class. No one said anything to us, not even the students. We just did whatever we had to do." Every now and then, she said there was a student, maybe an instructor,

57 Caillier interview; Bonnet interview; Fletcher Presidential Papers.

who greeted them. "Sometimes," she recalled, "but not very often."[58]

To combat the campus racism, black students drew strength from one another. They really had no choice but to band together because most of the campus was off limits to them. But being excluded from certain areas and events did not stop them from taking initiatives to ensure that they would obtain an education. That included providing their own bus transportation, particularly from the surrounding parishes, according to Caillier. The buses even doubled as their restaurant and activity center, a social gathering necessity because they were not allowed to eat in the campus cafeteria for a while. The drivers were also students.

When they finished for the day, they headed back to their respective towns and cities. In time, the Catholic Student Center became their epicenter. It was a significant turning point in their life because it offered them sanctuary. It offered them holy ground from which no one could evict.[59]

The black students could not do anything about their white classmates being given copies of the tests beforehand. But they could do something about the professors who flunked them because of their color. What they did was establish a grapevine, and passed the word on which professors they should not select for courses. They named names. On the other hand, there were professors who welcomed them into

58 James E. Lyons and Joanne Chesley, "Fifty Years After Brown: The Benefits and Tradeoffs for African American Educators and Students," *The Journal of Negro Education,* 73, no. 3 (2004): 310; Shelton Cobb and Rebecca Guilbeau Cobb interview.

59 Caillier interview; Shelton Cobb and Rebecca Guilbeau Cobb interviews.

their classes so much that they had to watch themselves before they took too many courses with these instructors—out of pure enjoyment. Rebecca Guilbeau Cobb remembers that was the case with psychology courses. There are memories also of two white professors in the music department who were kind to the African American students. When they had reached their course-taking limits with kind professors, it must have been an understood penalty that their time had run out.

Then the black students were forced to venture into classes where they were the butts of racial jokes and slurs. But they did not allow the campus to control—to destroy—them. Since Paul Breaux High School had been their alma mater, many of them knew one another and enjoyed a social life off campus at one another's houses. They engaged in activities that were beyond the racist reach of their campus life.[60]

By 1960, a lot had changed since 1950s when black students decided to be different than their predecessors—just like when they had decided they were not going to "burden" their parents financially anymore by attending Southern University. When he attended in 1960, Caillier estimated that there were eighteen black graduates from Paul Breaux High School, in addition to the ones from the nearby parishes, who had decided when it came to post-secondary education that Awe would go to school locally and we would make an impact here in Lafayette." While they knew SLI was open to blacks, Caillier said that they also knew it was Anot fully integrated, so we thought we would go there and integrate the school."[61]

60 Caillier interview; Shelton Cobb and Rebecca Guilbeau Cobb interviews.

61 James Caillier interview.

While desegregation led to the demise of the beanie, it reinforced black students' stake in the new university. They had not remained docile. What Shelton Cobb remembers the most about his SLI years, which began in 1960 when he transferred from Southern University, was that there was "a constant challenge, a constant struggle." In hindsight, his wife Rebecca Guilbeau Cobb viewed the struggles they encountered as opportunities that made them stronger and that better prepared them for the future. In learning to cope, these young students were able to ignore blatant acts of racism in their classrooms, including being ignored by their instructors, making lower grades than the white students, feeling unwelcome, and always understanding that there was only so far they could go.[62]

According to Dr. James Oliver, who's credited with building the university's computer science program, black students were there but only tolerated. "There was a big reluctance, on the part of both blacks and whites, to have very much human relations contact," he said in an interview.[63]

According to Dr. James Caillier, African Americans tolerated a lot in those days—a lot more than other communities would have. It had failed when it came to civil rights. He believes that at the time, any civil rights movement locally had been stymied by the fact that too many of the African American leaders had become "Toms," taking orders from the white power structure. These blacks were no different than

---

62 Caillier interview; Shelton and Rebecca Guilbeau Cobb interviews

63 Bonnet interview; James Oliver, interview by Michael J. Foret, June 30,1981. USL Oral History Project. Special Collections. Edith Garland Dupré Library. University of Louisiana at Lafayette, Lafayette, La.

others nationwide—their power base was rooted in their economic standing in their respective communities. In her dissertation, *The Travail and Triumph of a Southern Black Civil Rights Attorney: The Legal Career of Alexander Pierre Tureaud, 1899-1952,* Barbara Ann Worthy gives a clear purpose on how these subworlds existed within the race, and how their differences greatly impacted the black population's path on civil rights.[64]

When African Americans did not play by the rules infused by the white power structure and its beneficiaries and designees, there were consequences. According to Caillier, white students treated one of his African American buddies, who was studying engineering, to a severe beating for having had the audacity to dine off campus with a white female student. It was not something that Caillier heard through the grapevine. He witnessed his friend's bloody face and his bruises. They reported the incident to a dean but to no avail.

Caillier, himself, evaded potential harm by telling a "white" fib to the university police. He claimed that the white female student with whom he was sitting and chatting on a bench one evening was really black. Only by lying about the student's race did the campus police officer drive away from Catholic Student Center after stopping to inform them they could not sit together. Years prior to when Caillier, Cobb, and his wife Rebecca had registered as students, elders had drilled—and drummed—into their heads that they should be thankful to attend SLI. They all remember being constantly

64 Barbara Ann Worthy, *The Travail and Triumph of a Southern Black Civil Rights Attorney: The Legal Career of Alexander Pierre Tureaud, 1899-1952.* 1984, 1.

told by all forces, including black high school teachers and their parents, that whites had allowed them to attend SLI, and therefore, they better behave appropriately and accordingly. It seemed to be instilled that the whites were allowing them to attend "their" school. The other race's school. The youngsters wondered why was it not "their" school, too. On the other side of the racial lines, school officials enforced the message also. African Americans were lucky to attend the campus.

They were lucky to attend "their" school. The message was clear: It was never the black students' school. And the bottom line was that they were lucky—and that they should be thankful—to be there. Over and over, black students heard it was not "their" school.

Desegregation, therefore, did not mean integration.[65]

The recollections of the black students not only illustrate, but also confirm how harshly they were treated once they arrived. They learned quickly that aside from going to class and perhaps the library, they did not have full access to the campus. Noted Caillier: "The rest of the services were off limits." But such unspoken mandates were not exclusive to SLI. Other campuses experienced the same when their desegregation turn came up to bat.

And a lot of the feelings ranged from indifference to hatred. Dr. Milton Rickels, along with his wife Dr. Pat Rickels, considered themselves as friends of African Americans and went out of their way to support them. They were part of the inclusive gang that created the Human Relations Council with Oliver, black community activist Joe Dennis, and others. That did not stop them from being immune to feelings

65 Caillier interview; Shelton Cobb and Rebecca Guilbeau Cobb interviews.

wrought by racial hatred. Milton Rickels recalled that black students often felt excluded and could not belong to campus organizations. He cited one student in particular whom his heart ached for because she wanted to join the secretarial club, but she could not because she was not welcomed. "And it was a sorrow to her," he recalled. "And things like that angered me a great deal because it seemed so obviously unjust and so needlessly cruel."[66]

When a few of the African Americans formed a black team to participate in intramural sports and ended up beating several white teams, Caillier remembers being summoned to Dean Abel's office. Once again, the demanding question was there: Why? Before long, there were no more intramural sports on campus. The program simply ceased. While Abel does not mention the beanies or intramural sports incidents, his recollections included meeting with the African American male students regularly on Mondays to go over problems and help find solutions. He believed in righting wrongs, and this included correcting situations when instructors made African American sit in back of the classroom. According to Abel, he would pick up the phone in front of the black students and get the boss of the instructor on the phone, and let the supervisor know that the action should not happen again. While he elaborated on such occurrences, African American young men wanting to form a fraternity was not part of Abel's repertoire of memories.[67]

66 Dr. Milton Rickels, interview by Michael J. Foret, no date given. USL Oral History Project. Special Collections. Edith Garland Dupré Library. University of Louisiana at Lafayette, Lafayette, La.

67 Caillier Interivew; Glynn Abel.

But according to Caillier, the black students were given a difficult time when they tried to organize a black fraternity chapter of Alpha Phi Alpha. Once they managed to get a sponsor, they were told they had to make sure that the hierarchy of Alpha Phi Alpha national organization agreed that the local chapter would not allow any SLI white students to join.

When they told Abel that banning white students from the fraternity would violate the fraternity's national charter, it did not matter. Finally, the national organization agreed to recognize the SLI black students as an associate because it refused to allow the school to violate its charter. In his interview, Caillier contemplated on why SLI officials would even worry about white students becoming involved in the local black chapter. As he recalled, there was—maybe—one white student in whole country who had joined the Alphas at the time.[68]

When John Freeman came aboard as an African American student, SLI had been USL—the University of Southwestern Louisiana—for several years. Despite the name change, Freeman remembers that were many racial issues still in place and many barriers still existed for black students. Freeman recalled that there had been little change in regard to desegregation. "The only difference: we were the generation that caused the implementation," he said. He credits his generation, which began in 1964, with forcing visible change and refusing to bargain with blatant racism. According to Freeman, they developed tactics to deflect what they considered as offensive, such as the confederate battle flag, which was flown at school games. They organized an offensive attack, literally and figuratively,

68 Caillier interview.

and decided to become rebels and buy rebel flags of their own. When the SLI students cheered and waved their flags, the black students blew and wiped their noses with theirs. Before long, it cured the flag-waving confederacy. While intramural sports were still off-limits for black students, Freeman remembers that they organized teams and played off- campus. They refused to let the university dictate their lives. They relied on their upperclassmen for guidance but made their own tracks that ventured out into the city and resulted in desegregating restaurants and other local businesses.[69]

In the Edith Garland Dupré Library today, a large painting hangs of Christiana Gordon Smith, SLI's first graduate adorned in black cap and gown. A graduate student, Smith was nearly ready for a second degree when she entered SLI and later made history.

Like the plaintiffs in the 1954 lawsuit, and the black students who came afterwards, she too could not bear the financial costs of attending an out-of-town university. She chose to attend SLI. "The ice was already broken because there were other black students attending," said her sister Lela Gordon Mouton. According to Mouton, others speculated that Smith may not have endured as much racism as other black students did because she was a part-time student. But that changed graduation day when she walked down the aisle—alone—to receive her diploma because the white student, also named Smith, refused to walk with her. When her family members saw that she was by herself instead of walking two by two with another student, they quickly recognized that something was awry. Her sister recalled her demeanor: "She was walking with

69 John Freeman, interview by author, Lafayette, La., May 9, 2013.

her head up. She was walking as if to say, 'I don't care.' There was some kind of defiance." She had not let the snub bother her. Lela Gordon Mouton recalled Christiana's attitude went further. It was as if she was saying, "'I don't care if you don't walk me. I'm here to get my degree.' We can see the defiance in her as the graduates marched out," she said. Christiana Smith's defiance spoke also: "'If you're refusing to walk with me the shame is on you—not me.'"[70]

---

70 Mouton interview.

CHAPTER THREE

FIFTY YEARS AND THE AFTERMATH: REFLECTIONS AND REDEMPTION

> These four young people, along with their parents and their lawyers, challenged the restrictions and customs of southern society, a society defined by segregation—the separation of races.
>
> — Dr. Michael Martin

In the aftermath of the desegregation of the University of Louisiana at Lafayette, its golden anniversary in 2004 offered an opportunity for reflection and redemption. Everyone had tales, and some still had battle scars. But the reality of the occasion was that enough time had passed to publicly acknowledge the school's desegregation era: the early existence of African American on campus and the treatment—or mistreatment—they endured for becoming students at SLI. African American voices no longer had to be silent or ignored.

There were no more media blackouts. Both the university and the local media embraced the moment and the commemoration that marked its passing.

Perhaps indicative of the treatment African Americans received during SLI's desegregation was the fact that one of the four plaintiffs—Martha Jane Conway Bossett—refused to return for the school's golden anniversary of the historical occasion. "Fifty years later, she still had no desire to come," said University of Louisiana at Lafayette Alumni Association President Shawn Wilson in an interview. Her children were more forgiving, and came instead. A sibling represented Charles Singleton, who was ill. But the lawsuit's namesake Clara Dell Constantine Broussard attended, and so did plaintiff Shirley Taylor Gresham, who described the honors bestowed upon them during the anniversary as "unbelievable." Yet at the same time, Shirley Taylor Gresham was cognizant of what they had accomplished as young adults—the implications of their bold actions a half-century prior. "We put our necks out not only for ourselves, but for everyone in general who wanted to go to college," she said. Clara Dell Constantine Broussard noted that she was pleased that "what we did didn't go unnoticed." Others echoed similar sentiments. But it was obvious that these African American students were no longer invisible men and women as they once had been. It had taken half a century, but they were now visible. They could be seen.[71]

Some might consider it fate, but fifty years after desegregation and for the first time also, the university's Alumni Association president was an African American—Shawn Wilson, who today heads the Louisiana Department of Transportation and Development.

Wilson would also make campus history as the first student, black or white, to have the distinction of being both an Alumni Association and a Student Government Association president. During his Alumni presidency, which occurred when Dr. Ray Authement was president of the university, Wilson shared that he was determined to recognize the African American students who had paved the way for so many others during those early years. He was also determined that they would not suffer the same indignities as they had half a century earlier. One of those indignities in particular was being banned from the annual freshmen reception—an honored tradition—at the President's home. A campus newspaper, *The Vermilion,* noted that reception's occurrence on the front page of its September 17, 1954, issue—that first semester of desegregation. And although the campus story was but a few short paragraphs, it noted that the administration, faculty, and upperclassmen had attended and were there to greet the new students "in the garden of President Fletcher's home last Wednesday evening." The headline stated, "Annual

71 Christine Payton, "Ceremony Recognizes Desegregation Anniversary: Four students honored for initiating change in 1954," December 17, 2004, http://anisette.ucs.louisiana.edu/Advancement/PRNS/news/2004/352.shtml (accessed May 21, 2018).

President's Reception Welcomes Freshman Students." Perhaps an asterisk should have denoted which freshmen students because the welcome mat was not in place for the first African Americans students. But fifty years later during the anniversary celebration, Alumni President Wilson would ensure the black students' anniversary return included an overdue freshmen reception. Unlike his predecessor Fletcher, President Ray Authement hosted the reception for the former students at his campus home in 2004. Authement also bestowed honorary degrees for the designated four plaintiffs, as well as for the NAACP Secretary Helma Constantine, whose daughter Clara Dell's name appeared on the landmark lawsuit. Also during the fiftieth anniversary, according to Wilson, tales of blatant racism were shared by those who had witnessed—and who had endured—them firsthand. Among such stories recalled was the one about Dr. Fletcher spitting every time he passed a student when she greeted him.[72]

That lack of publicity played a role in 1954 after officials opted for a news blackout when the college was ordered to admit black students. That is why primary sources are few, and research has been difficult for historians like Michael G. Wade, who is writing a book on the desegregation of Louisiana's higher learning institutions. Wade, a former student of what was the University of Southwestern Louisiana in his day and a history professor at the Appalachian State University, acknowledged the blackout in an interview with the local media. "At the time, they were having to deal with an enormous white backlash that intensified after the *Brown* decision," said

72 Wilson interview; "Annual President's Reception Welcomes Freshman Students," *The Vermilion*, September 17, 1954.

Wade who also participated in the 2004 anniversary symposium. "For reasons that had to do with segregationist politics as much as anything else, the university did whatever it could to discourage publicity and to minimize the giving out of information. As a result, very little was put down."[73]

In his essay, "Four Who Would: *Constantine v. Southwestern Louisiana Institute* (1954) and the Desegregation of Louisiana's State Colleges" Wade was pragmatic in defining desegregation at SLI. "In some respects the desegregation of SLI is unavoidably a story of narrow-mindedness and of bigotry," he wrote. "But it is also a human saga of individual courage, magnanimity, and the leadership of a community pulling together to do what the law required, peaceably and with a small measure of equanimity. They did so reluctantly and imperfectly. But they did it." He also acknowledged the importance of African Americans' role in the desegregation saga: both their contribution and their courage. According to Wade, these two attributes should not be "underestimated." However, in making his point, Wade calls attention to the different skin tones within the race by singling out "black" in quotations from the word people. He describes the contributions as coming from " 'black' people of all hues."[74]

According to Dr. Michael S. Martin, then assistant professor of history and later the director of the Center for Louisiana Studies, the desegregation of SLI had "national implications," which significance was being realized by historians. "These four young people, along with their parents and their lawyers,

---

73 "In Search of History," http://www.raginpagin.com/louisiana/showthread.php?1668-Separate-but- equal&p'20726.

74 Michael G. Wade, 80.

challenged the restrictions and customs of southern society, a society defined by segregation—the separation of races," said Martin, who also served as an anniversary organizer.[75]

Today, on the University of Louisiana at Lafayette campus at the corner of St. Mary Boulevard and Rex Street, stand four Pillars of Progress—the Pillar of Courage, Pillar of Justice, Pillar of Faith and the Pillar of Knowledge. They uphold a covered area where students wait for the school's bus transit services. Dedicated in 2004, the pillars commemorate not only the school's fiftieth anniversary of desegregation but also the fiftieth anniversary of *Brown v. Board of Education of Topeka*. While it also "pays homage" to the school's first African American students, the marker notes that it "acknowledges" all those who "contributed to the Civil Rights Movement." The tribute was erected by the Alumni Association as part of the university's presentation of honorary degrees to the desegregation's plaintiffs on December 18, 2004.[76]

The four pillars represent "the four who would," with a plaque on each bearing one of the names of the plaintiffs in *Constantine v. SLI*. Underneath, in alphabetical order and in two columns, on each pillar, are also the names of the students who attended the first semester.

The first, the Pillar of Courage bearing the name of Clara Dell Constantine followed by the names of eighteen students, states: "They taught future generations about courage with their determination to attend SLI despite the uncertainty of

75 Michael S. Martin, Speech, 50th Anniversary, 2004.

76 Pillars of Progress, St. Mary Boulevard and Rex Street, University of Louisiana at Lafayette campus.

how they would be treated in an academic and social environment that was unfamiliar to them."[77]

The second, the Pillar of Justice, bears the names of Martha Jane Conway and eighteen more students. It notes: "Their actions ensured that any qualified individual could attend SLI and led to the desegregation of other universities in the South." The Pillar of Faith, the third pillar, bearing Shirley Taylor's name and additional eighteen students' names, states, "They demonstrated that with faith—people, systems and institutions can change for the betterment of all." And the fourth pillar, the Pillar of Knowledge, bearing Charles Vincent Singleton's name and twenty students, states: "By their efforts, they made a lasting statement about the value of higher education and the empowerment it provides." Two of the plaintiffs' names, Constantine and Singleton, do not also appear in any of the two-column listings on the four pillars as the names of Conway and Taylor do. In total, there are seventy- four names listed on the four pillars.[78]

A large marker, attached to a nearby wall, provides the context for the commemoration. It notes that on September 15, 1953, the four students attempted to enroll at SLI, and how a year later, on September 10, 1954, the school became "the first all-white, state-supported college in the Deep South to desegregate" when seventy-six African American students registered. The marker notes that there were difficult times ahead even though SLI accomplished desegregation "without the violence" other southern schools endured. "But the turmoil

77 Ibid.

78 Pillars of Progress, St. Mary Boulevard and Rex Street, University of Louisiana at Lafayette campus.

on SLI's campus took its toll by mid-term," it concludes, "the number of African American students at SLI had markedly decreased." A second marker, underneath the first, explains the significance of the "Four Pillars of Progress."[79]

While the actions of "the four who would" may have not been documented much over the years, there is no doubt of the power they held. University President E. Joseph Savoie acknowledged that power in 2015 when the Helma B. Constantine Forum was dedicated during the open house for the campus's new Student Union. According to the campus website, he said that her "efforts to help her daughter achieve her dream of higher education was a cause that 'was just, and her conviction was strong.'"[80]

"By actively seeking a better life for her children, Helma Constantine and others ensured that justice was given a chance to prevail," Savoie noted, "and that future generations would not be denied equal opportunities." Attending the ceremony was her daughter Joyce Constantine Henson who noted how committed her mother was to learning. "My mother was stubborn, and felt that the only way up from poverty was education," Henson said. "She insisted that we all get an education of some kind. And, every young person that she talked to, she would ask, 'Where are you in school?' It was very important to her."[81]

---

79 Ibid. See also Christine Payton.

80 "Visitors explore new Student Union on UL Lafayette campus." News. September 14, 2015. https://louisiana.edu/news-events/news/20150914/visitors-explore-new-student-union-ul-lafayette- campus(accessed May 21, 2018).

81 Ibid.

The legacy of 1954 lives on. There is no doubt that these four students and others challenged what was, what had been, and what was to come. And in doing so, they redefined history—a history that was real—and rerouted the destiny of their descendants.

CONCLUSION

WITH, WITHOUT INCIDENT?

> It was just as brutal as the other schools, but without all the fanfare.
>
> — Dr. James Caillier

There are two schools of opinion in regard to how desegregation took place at SLI, whether it occurred "with" or "without" incident. The significance those terms hold has become a matter of interpretation. But the question is can there be only a single correct answer, or do both interpretations hold ground?

For many, "with incident" means the large, bold block letters that blasted across *The Birmingham News* on the evening of October 1, 1962: "MEREDITH ENROLLS AT OLE MISS UNDER BAYONETS; RIOTS RENEWED." All letters, all words were capitalized. Underneath the blazing headline to the right on the front page was a sub-headline in italics with smaller letters and words: "Two killed; 112 arrested." It was a newspaper front page that would gain infamy, forever etched in the public's mind. That was what the nation thought about when it remembered the desegregation of Ole Miss. Remembrance was from afar, including in Lafayette, Louisiana, and years later, when officials of SLI—by then, the University of Southwestern Louisiana, or USL—and others cared to reflect, and compare both incidents. Always, and without hesitation, they would recall that the SLI desegregation had paled in comparison, and despite the number of African American students who entered that first 1954 fall semester, the enrollment had been "without incident" The two-word phrase, or similar text, had come to symbolize the desegregation of the school. But as Robert Weaver noted, there is a tendency to exaggerate progress and minimize gains, and overall, incidents become a matter of perception.[82]

The beanie incident is one example. Witnesses saw determined young African American men who defied Southwestern Louisiana Institute's desegregation script. These were bold young men who refused to play the roles given them. Instead they wrote their own lines. "It was a general agreement," Caillier recalled, "if you come and you don't create any problems, and you go to class and go home, you're okay. You're

82 "Integrating Ole Miss: A Civil Rights Milestone," http://microsites.jfklibrary.org/olemiss/home (accessed May 9, 2013); "Meredith Enrolls at Ole Miss," *The Birmingham News* front page, Digital History ID 4186, http://www.digitalhistory.uh.edu/disp_textbook.cfm?smtID=8&psid=4186&filepath=http://www.digitalhistory. uh.edu/primarysources_upload/images/Meredith_Enrolls_at_Ole_Miss_LG.jpg (accessed May 20, 2018); Robert Weaver.

okay." The young men decided they were not okay with the status quo—they were not okay with an administration that controlled the message in order to control and ensure a skewed reality. Fifty years later and beyond, that administration was confident that it had succeeded because, without shame or regret and, or redemption, university officials and followers were able to firmly inject "without incident" into the SLI desegregation narrative wherever the story went and whatever historical discussion it brought forth in the decades to come.[83]

The lack of media coverage was obvious during desegregation—obvious because little documentation exists of what happened. But fifty years later, media coverage, including the campus news service, kept the public abreast of the anniversary celebration activities.

They, too, took time to reflect on the five decades that had passed, and what had happened in 1954 and after. And they, too, peppered the phrase, "without incident," throughout their news copy. They also contemplated on why the historic event occurred without incident and came up with several possibilities. First, the campus newsfeed surmised that desegregation "occurred relatively smooth." And noted that was "a matter of record." One theory devoted several bullet points to Fletcher alone, including his lack of publicity and no-comment stance. According to the campus media, he was also cited for encouraging cooperation. Also noted were his orders to Registrar Bonnet on documenting the number of African American students. Yet today, a three-page list of the students has been saved from the era. What is interesting was that post-desegregation interviews recalled that Fletcher

83 Caillier interview.

toured the state trying to garner support for what was to befall his campus. The campus media notes that he reached out to "influential society members."

And aside from Fletcher, it was also noted that the Louisiana Human Relations Council assisted in bringing calm to any potential storm, and that led to "without incident." Then according to the media, there was Rev. Alexander O. Sigur who was commended because his Catholic Student Center became a safe haven for the races to meet and mingle. And last but not least, the Dean of Men Glynn Abel was given due respect for promoting the races to work together. But for some black students, these suppositions were mere fantasies and factually inconsistent during their stay on campus.

As mentioned previously, the university gained historical honors as being the first southern school to desegregate by default. Yet we know that it was by happenstance that this honor was bestowed upon the college campus. It was an honor that they did not boast about in the beginning. Instead officials took stern action to ensure they controlled any dissent they could imagine. Therefore, African American students found themselves as invisible students, barely acknowledged as equals. But these students were strong-willed and determined to succeed against the many obstacles put before them, despite being barely adults. How did they endure staying on their school bus because the campus was off-limits to them except for their classes and a few other places? How did they feel being on the bus daily before they were welcome at the student Catholic Center? What was it like to not be invited to the annual freshmen reception at the President's house? What message did that send? What feelings of welcome did that foster, especially since it was published in the school newspaper to let them know that there been an event that they were not welcomed? How were officials able to keep the black students corralled together as if they were cattle, preventing them from venturing out? And for these young people, back-stabbing words did not break their bones, but hastened departures for those of them who had enough. Some African American students did not allow themselves to be subjected to such indignities. They refused to be subjected to what they considered was inhumane treatment. They refused to go to SLI, and some even refused to share their stories of why they circumvented torment and trauma.

For those African American students who succumbed to desegregation even though they knew they were not part of the equation, the words "without incident" are hollow indeed even though they were not victims or witnesses to the horrors that other desegregation suits brought forth. They did not have the bloodshed that was later visited upon other campuses.

And no one was left dead. They did not endure what could be termed as "with incident," but they left with mental scars that were just as painful. The SLI desegregation did not garner national attention because officials were so intent on keeping their circumstances quiet, so much that we witness with the beanie incident that some white community residents and business owners did not even realize that the university had been desegregated. The SLI officials had succeeded in controlling the narrative of the event, and for that, they can be recognized and accept the accolades that no one was injured or killed at SLI during desegregation. But when it comes to accepting accolades for denying truth, then we must state the facts and know that both sides of the equation must be recorded. There were no James Merediths. This was a community that preferred to alter reality than suffer consequences. And in doing so, they altered the reality of the black power base. For some, it was a sham. But it was not something new. These power bases existed elsewhere. We expect the same was in Lafayette because Alfred McZeal recalled the orders he was given: to blatantly lie when questioned about the lunch counter that refused to seat African Americans. He was forced to pretend that the counter had been integrated when he knew the store did not even allow his own children to be served.[84]

But to thwart action, and what could have become dangerous, the white community leaders called upon their black community leaders, and they did exactly what they had to do. They helped to halt a breakdown of the system. They rallied to make sure Dr. King would not come to the community, and if he and other civil rights protestors did, then everything would be in place. To ensure the safety and solidity of their employment, African Americans like Alfred McZeal would quash any rumors of segregation in local lunch counters and bus stations. The naked truth was too damning for the community. And leaders ensuring a state of calm displayed the power they beheld. Those times, those years, allowed such power to proceed across the South, which included lynching and the meaningless loss of lives. But that power was allowed to succeed as long as it was not publicized. New days were coming, and documentation brought an unmasking of the tales that needed to be told. No was willing to keep hiding

84 McZeal interview.

that power. And perhaps no one was willing to go head-to-toe with what may have become an all-out battle.[85]

Dawn was over, and we find a new day, and in that day, the truth must be told and shared. "Without incident", as a result, becomes a matter of reality subject to interpretation. There were no physical attacks, but battle lines were drawn, and the ramifications of the SLI desegregation endured beyond the fifty-year anniversary. Its impact had not been released from the minds of those who refuse to accept change on both sides. For those African Americans who had suffered, who had walked miles to get their education, who had suffered verbal attacks, but who had stood their grounds, it was not an accommodating role to play in history. Yet they had endured hatred for making a difference in their lives and the lives of the generations to follow. Therefore to say, the desegregation was "without incident" may be considered an insult to African Americans who were treated with disrespect, or not even acknowledged. That is the legacy that must also be questioned. And perhaps at the one hundredth anniversary, an apology may be rendered—an acknowledgment that enables a truce.[86]

The university, a small college at the time then, had fought desegregation. It had fought desegregation every step of the way. And if it could have succeeded without desegregation, it surely would have done so. President Abraham Lincoln said if he could have saved the Union without freeing a single slave, he would have done so. This remark and supposition may seem shocking to some, but the same argument could be held in regard to the desegregation of SLI. If the officials

85 McZeal interview.

86 Ibid.; Dennis interview.

could have accepted desegregation without admitting a single black student, they most likely would have at the time. They desegregated because they had no choice. SLI would not have welcomed black students if it did not have to welcome them. And when it was finally forced to desegregate because of a court order, it made sure that the African American students understood that they were still not welcome. There was never any doubt that white leaders hoped their disdain would discourage more African Americans from registering. And in that aspect, they were correct and successful.[87]

In reviewing the desegregation, we must say that "without incident" is a matter of interpretation. It is a matter of perception. The fact that it occurred does not mean it was a willing matter, or that the school should be praised for its actions. SLI desegregated by force and by default. Without acknowledging its past, it is receiving acclaim as the first for something that the school had previously fought to prevent. And in this case, something it did not want. But now that history, that legacy would once again call to mind *1984.* Today, such efforts would be understood as rebranding, and for many, there is nothing wrong with that.

Everyone wants to be the first, and when entitled to become the first, then they consider action taken as right—correct, ethical. Remaining desegregation actors will not be alive in 2054 to see what happens to the campus that became the first in the South to desegregate. It will be interesting to see what the university celebrates then.

Today, it is a fact that there were no James Merediths, no bayonets, no riots even though Dr. James Cailler's friend

87 http://www.digitalhistory.uh.edu/documents/documents_p2.cfm2doc=185

was bloodied and bruised for dining with a white female. But what mattered more than the beating was the atmosphere that condoned such behavior. For the African American students, the problem was not so much the action taken, but the action not taken. Just like words not spoken. That is why there are no regrets from black students who share their stories today, including the retired educators Shelton and Rebecca Cobb. However, as the former president of the Lafayette Parish School Board, Shelton Cobb has reason to worry that days of discrimination may be sneaking back into the school system. By minimizing and shunning publicity as the first campus to desegregate during those beginning years, SLI may have forfeited an opportunity for more pages in history on its significant role because it utilized the minimalist approach. But in doing so, school officials may have minimized injuries, even deaths. Despite a chapter on school desegregation and white flight in Lafayette Parish, sociologist Stephen J. Caldas and educator Carl L. Bankston III do not even note that distinction in their earlier book, *A Troubled Dream: The Promise and Failure of School Desegregation in Louisiana,* even though Caldas was noted as a member of the faculty when the book was published in 2002. The only historical context the authors noted about the university was that its first black student was admitted "without protest from the white community" after *Brown*. But history's negligence of SLI as a history- maker does present irony: Had their world imploded because of publicity at the time of desegregation, SLI officials—and the campus itself—would have survived in infamy. The question becomes would that have been better or worse than SLI President Fletcher's idea of coexistence and racial harmony?[88]

For those blacks who attended the early years, there was little difference between SLI and the schools which later exploded into riots and bloodshed. For those who attended the Lafayette campus, the fallout was just the same. Without a focus on education, African Americans agree that they would not have kept going to SLI because of its racial cruelness.

But at the time, they were not willing to let anything stand in their way. The indignities that they experienced were no different than the ones forthcoming—the "with incident" ones heavily publicized by the media. For now—as it was back then, there is no free pass for SLI when it comes to the desegregation of Southern institutions. For African American students, there was no difference between the desegregation at SLI and the desegregation elsewhere. According to Caillier and other African Americans, desegregation at SLI was not as unique as heralded, nor was it any different than the ones that made blazing headlines later. "It was just as brutal as the other schools," says Dr. Caillier, "but without all the fanfare."[89]

88 Shelton Cobb and Rebecca Guilbeau Cobb interviews; Caillier interview; Carl Bankston III and Stephen J. Caldas. *A Troubled Dream: The Promise and Failure of School Desegregation in Louisiana.* Nashville: Vanderbilt University Press, 2002, 112.

89 Shelton Cobb and Rebecca Guilbeau Cobb interviews; Caillier interview.

BIBLIOGRAPHY

Primary Sources

Abel, Glynn. Interview by Michael J. Foret, June 24, 1981. USL Oral History Project. Special Collections. Edith Garland Dupré Library. University of Louisiana at Lafayette, Lafayette, La.

Bienvenu, Jr., C. Thomas., Interview by author, St. Martinville, La., April 12, 2012, Recording, in author's possession.

Bonnet, James Stewart. Interview by Michael J. Foret. No date given. USL Oral History Project. Special Collections. Edith Garland Dupré Library. University of Louisiana at Lafayette, Lafayette, La.

Broussard, Clara Dell Constantine. Obituary Program, March 1, 2012.

Caillier, James. Interview by author. Lafayette, La., March 3, 2013. Recording, in author's possession.

Caillier, James. Biographical Profile: James Allen Caillier, President Emeritus of the University of Louisiana System.

Clara Dell Constantine, et al v. The Southwestern Louisiana Institute, et al. 4401 Civil Action. January 4, 1954.

Clara Dell Constantine, et al v. The Southwestern Louisiana Institute, et al. 4401 Civil Action. Permanent Injunction, July 19, 1954.

Cobb, Shelton and Rebecca Guilbeau Cobb, Interviews by author, Lafayette, La. March 3, 2013. Recording, in author's possession.

Dennis, Joe. Interview by author. Lafayette, La. March 13, 2012. Recording, in author's possession.

"Federal Judges Order SLI To Admit Negro Students: Court Rules Equal Accommodations Not Available to Race in Area." *The Daily (Lafayette) Advertiser.* April 23, 1954.

Freeman, John. Interview by author. Lafayette, La. March 13, 2012, May 8, 2013. Recording, in author's possession.

Haynes, J. K. Interview by Doris White. January 20, 1976. Location unknown. Transcript. https://library.louisiana.edu/collections/university-archives-manuscripts/acadiana- manuscripts-collections/miscellaneous-97(accessed May 23, 2018)

"Integrating Ole Miss: A Civil Rights Milestone," http://microsites.jfklibrary.org/olemiss/home (accessed May 9, 2013)

James, Carlton. Oral History Collection. The University of Louisiana at Lafayette Libraries, University Archives and Acadiana Manuscripts Collection, University of Louisiana at Lafayette, Col. 161, Box 4, Tape 1.

Martin, Michael. Speech, 50th Anniversary, 2004.

McZeal, Sr., Alfred. Interview by author. Lafayette, La. March 3, 2012. Recording, in author's possession.

Mouton, Lela Gordon. Interview by author. Lafayette/Carencro, La. May 8, 2013. Notes, in author's possession.

Oliver, James. Interview by Michael J. Foret. June 30,1981. USL Oral History Project. Special Collections. Edith Garland Dupré Library. University of Louisiana at Lafayette, Lafayette, La.

Rickels, Dr. Milton. Interview by Michael J. Foret. No date given. USL Oral History Project. Special Collections. Edith Garland Dupré Library. University of Louisiana at Lafayette, Lafayette, La.

Riehl, Joseph A. Interview by Michael J. Foret. June 24, 1981. USL Oral History Project, Special Collections, Edith Garland Dupré Library. University of Louisiana at Lafayette, Lafayette, La.

Trice, Lowell M. "Dixie Governors Say Desegregation Must be Solved on Local Level," *The Plain Dealer*, August 19, 1955, Vol. 57, Issue 33.

Wilson, Shawn. Interview by author. Lafayette, La. March 12, 2012. Recording, In author's possession.

Secondary Sources

Caldas, Stephen J. and Carl L. Bankston III. *A Troubled Dream: The Promise and Failure of School Desegregation in Louisiana.* Nashville: Vanderbilt University Press, 2002.

Caldas, Stephen J. and Carl L. Bankston III. *Forced to Fail: The Paradox of School Desegregation.* Westpart, CT: Praeger Publishers, 2005.

Chafe, William H. *Civilities and Civil Rights: Greensboro, North Carolina, and the Black Struggle for Freedom.* Oxford: Oxford University Press, 1980.

Clark, E. Culpepper. *The Schoolhouse Door: Segregation's Last Stand at the University of Alabama.* Tuscaloosa: University of Alabama Press, 1993.

Douglass, Frederick. "What the Black Man Wants." April 1865. http://utc.iath.virginia.edu/africam/afspfdat.html(accessed May 30, 2018)

Eagles, Charles W. *The Price of Defiance: James Meredith and the Integration of Old Miss.* Chapel Hill: University of North Carolina Press, 2009.

Emanuel, Rachel L. and Alexander P. Tureaud, Jr. *A More Noble Cause: A.P. Tureaud and the Struggle for Civil Rights in Louisiana.* Baton Rouge: Louisiana State University Press, 2011.

Fairclough, Adam. *Race & Democracy: The Civil Rights Struggle in Louisiana 1915-1972.* Athens: University of Georgia Press, 1995.

Finley, Keith M. "Southern Opposition to Civil Rights in the United States Senate: A Tactical and Ideological Analysis, 1938-1965." PhD diss., Louisiana State University and Agricultural and Mechanical College, 2003.

Foote, Ruth. "History-maker Eager to See History Made." *The Advocate,* January 19, 2009. http://www.louisiana.edu/news-events/news/20040901/50-years-later-desegregation-s li. accessed May 8, 2013.

Griffin, Harry Lewis. *The Attakapas Country: A History of Lafayette Parish, Louisiana.*

Gretna: Pelican Publishing Co., 1959. Lyons, James E. Lyons and Joanne Chesley. "Fifty Years After Brown: The Benefits and Tradeoffs for African American Educators and Students." *The Journal of Negro Education*, 73, no. 3, 2004.

Klarman, Michael J. *From Jim Crow to Civil Rights: The Supreme Court and the Struggle for Racial Equality.* Oxford University Press, 2004.

Kluger, Richard. *Simple Justice: The History of Brown v. Board of Education and Black America's Struggle for Equality.* New York: Vintage Books, 1975, 2004.

"Meredith Enrolls at Ole Miss." *The Birmingham News* front page. Digital History ID 4186. http://www.digitalhistory.

uh.edu/disp_textbook.cfm?smtID=8&psid=4186&file-path= http://www.digitalhistory.uh.edu/primarysources_upload/images/Meredith_Enrolls_at_Ole_Miss_LG.jpg. Accessed May 20, 2018.

Southwestern Louisiana Institute (SLI),."University History: General." UL Lafayette website, http://anisette.ucs.louisiana.edu/AboutUs/History/General.shtml. Accessed May 9, 2013.

Thames, Kathleen. "A Look Back at 100 Years." *La Louisiane*. Fall 2000.

Wade, Michael G. "Four Who Would: The Desegregation of Louisiana's State Colleges/ Constantine v. Southwestern Louisiana Institute (1954) and the Desegregation of Louisiana's State Colleges," in *Higher Education and the Civil Rights Movement: White Supremacy, Black Southerners, and College Campuses*, edited by Peter Wallenstein. Gainesville: University Press of Florida, 2008.

Wallenstein, Peter, ed. *Higher Education and the Civil Rights Movement: White Supremacy, Black Southerners, and College Campuses*. Gainesville: University Press of Florida, 2008.

White, Doris Morein. "The Louisiana Civil Rights Movement: Pre-Brown Period, 1936- 1954." Master's thesis, University of Southwestern Louisiana, 1976.

Worthy, Barbara Ann. "The Travail and Triumph of a Southern Black Civil Rights Attorney: The Legal Career of Alexander Pierre Tureaud, 1899-1952." Dissertation, Tulane University, 1984.

Foote, Ruth Anita. Bachelor of Arts, University of Southwestern Louisiana, Spring 1982; Master of Arts, University of Louisiana at Lafayette, Summer 2018

Major: History

Title of Thesis: "just as brutal... but without all the fanfare": African American Students, Racism, and Defiance during the Desegregation of Southwestern Louisiana Institute, 1954-1964

Thesis Director: Dr. Robert Carriker

Pages in Thesis: 79; Words in Abstract: 202

ABSTRACT

In 1954, Southwestern Louisiana Institute (now the University of Louisiana at Lafayette) became the first undergraduate school in the Deep South to desegregate. Its acclaim as the first, however, was promoted only because it lost as a defendant in *Clara Dell Constantine et al. v. Southwestern Louisiana Institute et al.* What occurred then, and the indignities experienced by African American students during that first decade has never been fully documented. The black experience was figuratively and literally blacked out.

African American students found themselves receiving lower grades in class than their white counterparts. Social events banned them, and school services denied access. To cope with racism, they drew strength by supporting one another, developing a grapevine, establishing their own social network, and most of all, keeping focused on their education.

But not everyone was against them. Some whites risked their reputation, and became their brother's keeper.

The four Pillars of Progress, commemorating the fiftieth anniversaries of SLI's desegregation and *Brown* in 2004, stand today as a campus testament to that era. But what remains at odds is whether the desegregation of SLI was "without incident." That still remains a matter of interpretation and depends on whom is being asked and who answers.

BIOGRAPHICAL SKETCH

Ruth Foote, the daughter of Gloria Smyer Foote and the late Joel L. Foote, Sr., was born in Augsburg, Germany. She grew up as an *army brat* in Washington, Germany and Georgia. As a child, she had never experienced segregation and racism until her father moved the family to Louisiana in the late 1960s before retiring from the military. During the summer before her senior year at Lafayette High School, she first attended the University of Louisiana at Lafayette through its Early Admission Program. In 1982, she graduated with a B.A. in English-Journalism.

She works full-time as the grants director for SMILE Community Action Agency.

She is also an award-winning journalist, and enjoys freelancing for *The Advocate* newspaper.

In 2015, she was honored with the University of Louisiana at Lafayette's Department of History, Geography and Philosophy's *Jamie Guilbeau Award for Public History*.

She has presented her thesis research at the Phi Alpha Theta History Honor Society's Annual Regional Meeting (Hammond, Louisiana), Louisiana Historical Association's 57th Annual Meeting (Lafayette, Louisiana) and the 8th Annual La. Studies Conference (Natchitoches, Louisiana).

She is a member of the university's Phi Alpha Theta's Epsilon Xi Chapter, and in 2015, served on its Editorial Committee for *Clio's Quill.* In 2016, she presented "The Desegregation of Southwestern Louisiana Institute (SLI)" at the South Regional Library in Lafayette, Louisiana.

Made in the USA
Columbia, SC
12 May 2025

57758292R00061